BACH
an extraordinary life

DAVID MORONEY

For Robina,
this little book about
a Big Subject!
Affectionately,

[signature]

Berkeley, 3rd Feb 2002.

The Associated Board of
the Royal Schools of Music

First published in 2000 by
The Associated Board of the Royal Schools of Music (Publishing) Limited
14 Bedford Square, London WC1B 3JG, United Kingdom

© 2000 Davitt Moroney
The rights of Davitt Moroney to be identified as the author of this work have been asserted
in accordance with the Copyright, Designs and Patents Act 1988

This edition first published in 2000 by ABRSM (Publishing) Limited
This format and design © 2000 The Associated Board of the Royal Schools of Music

ISBN 1 86096 190 8

AB 2762

A CIP catalogue for this book is available from The British Library.
Design by Geoff Wadsley.
Printed in England by Redwood Books, Trowbridge, Wiltshire.

ACKNOWLEDGEMENTS

We are grateful to the following for permission to reproduce photographs:

Front cover: Detail from an anonymous copy of Bach portrait by Haussmann. By permission of
The British Library and the Hirsch Collection.

Front and back cover: Extract from an engraving of Thomaskirche and Thomasschule,
Leipzig, by Johann Georg Schreiber, dated 1735, from the original in the Archiv für Kunst
und Geschichte, Berlin. By permission of AKG Photo, London.

Back cover: Bach's wine goblet. By kind permission of the Bachhaus, Eisenach.

p. 42: The first page of Prelude I from *The Well-Tempered Clavier*, Book 1. By permission of the
Hulton Getty Picture Library, London.

p. 62: Bach's signature as cantor at the Thomaskirche, Leipzig, from an original in the Archiv
für Kunst und Geschichte, Berlin. By permission of AKG Photo, London.

PLATES
Interior of the palace church (*Himmelsburg*) at Weimar. Gouache by Christian Richter
    (*d.* 1667), *c.*1660. By permission of AKG Photo, London.
Autograph score of the beginning of the first movement of the Brandenburg Concerto No. 2
    in F major, BWV 1047, probably written in Cöthen 1717–18. By permission of AKG Photo,
    London.
Autograph score of the first movement of the Sonata in G minor for solo violin, BWV 1001,
    Cöthen 1720. By permission of the Lebrecht Collection, London.
'Still-life with Smoking Utensils' by Jean Baptiste Simeon Chardin (1699–1779), *c.*1760–63.
    Oil on canvas. From the original in the Musée du Louvre, Paris. By permission of AKG
    Photo, London/Erich Lessing.
Engraving of the St Thomaskirche and Thomasschule, Leipzig, by Johann Gottfried Krügner
    (1684–1769), dated 1723. By permission of AKG Photo, London.
Anonymous copy of Bach portrait by Haussmann. By permission of The British Library.
'The Leipzig Kuchengarten' (in the suburb of Gaststätte), drawn in 1746. By permission of
    the Lebrecht Collection, London.
Engraving showing various ophthalmology instruments, eye growths, a cataract operation
    and other eye defects by R. Parr, *c.*1743–5. By permission of the Wellcome Library,
    London.
Autograph of page 19 of the manuscript of *The Art of Fugue*, BWV 1080, Leipzig 1748–9, from
    the original in the Staatsbibliothek, Berlin. By permission of AKG Photo, London.

Bonae Artis Cultorem Habeas

Bach's signature to a canon,
1 March 1749

Foreword

This biography is intended to be accessible to readers who love Bach's music, buy records and go to concerts. Full archival references concerning all the incidents mentioned here can be found in the sources given at the back of the book. I happily acknowledge my debt to these Bach scholars; they have published the material on which this book is based.

The German texts of the original documents can be found in the three volumes of *Bach-Dokumente* (*B-Dok*). Many of them may be found in *The New Bach Reader* (*NBR*); in general I have used this standard English translation, by permission of the publisher. Another anthology containing a somewhat different selection of texts is Gilles Cantagrel's *Bach en son temps* (*BEST*). This book will have achieved what it set out to do if it encourages readers to open these five volumes.

BWV refers to the 1998 revision of the *Bach-Werke-Verzeichnis*, the standard catalogue of Bach's works.

This volume was written in English but first published in French and Portuguese. I would particularly like to thank the people who were instrumental in bringing it into being. René Martin and Miguel Lobo Antunes first had the idea for this text; without their enthusiasm, it would never have been written. The expert eye of Hélène Ménissier improved many details. Dennis Collins enhanced the text considerably by his close and attentive reading. Dominique Montel kindly prepared the musical illustrations from examples of Bach's own handwriting.

DM, Paris, 1 January 2000

Contents

CHAPTER ONE

Son, Orphan, Brother, Organ Student
(1685–1703)

He, the deepest savant of contrapuntal arts (and even artifices),
knew how to subordinate art to beauty.

Anonymous text, 27 February 1788[1]

Johann Sebastian Bach was born on 21 March 1685 in Eisenach, a small town in Thuringia in central Germany. He was born into a most extraordinary network of professional musicians, the greatest dynasty in the history of European music. Nearly 80 musicians named Bach are known, all in the same family.[2] More than half of them were organists and quite a few were born or worked in or close to Eisenach. It would have been remarkable if Johann Sebastian had followed any path in life other than music. He became an organist, *Capellmeister* and cantor, like dozens of other members of the Bach family.

Organists and church musicians were not the only thing for which Eisenach was famous. Bach's first school, the town's Lateinschule, had also been Martin Luther's school for over three years. The great Protestant reformer had left the town in 1501, but returned and preached a sermon in St George's church in 1521, three months after being excommunicated by the Pope. He was arrested but was able to go into hiding in the Wartburg, the Eisenach castle. In the space of ten weeks he produced there his famous translation of the New Testament from Greek into German, one of the most important books in the history of German cultural identity.[3] Lutheranism was as integral a part of the Bach family's tradition as was music. In the early sixteenth century, the founder of the musical branch of the dynasty, the baker Veit Bach, had been a Lutheran.

However, this double heritage, musical and Lutheran, does not explain why Johann Sebastian became so much greater a musician than his elder brother, for example, who had all the same family advantages, the same religious background and had, moreover, been a pupil of the famous organist Johann Pachelbel (1653–1706). In the Bach family, personal style was largely lost in the mass of competent music-making. So why did Johann Sebastian's individuality burst out with an almost violent force, almost as if his first task was to outdo the other members of the family? The answer lies partly in the fact that he was able first to digest and assimilate what he learnt from his numerous excellent teachers and models and then to rethink their musical styles into something quite new. As a result, he achieved immeasurably more than any other member of the family before him. What little we know of his personality also shows several characteristics that, when taken together with and added to the family and religious background, make up an irresistible cocktail. Two features that must have helped the young Johann Sebastian make rapid progress are easy to identify: his voracious musical curiosity and appetite, and his healthily vigorous ambition. Yet it is two further characteristics that offer the essential keys to Bach's later achievements: his exceptional intelligence and his remarkable aptitude for hard work.

Among these aspects of his personality, writers have often dwelt on his impressively rational, analytical intelligence. Indeed, this side is so often stressed that some people are put off by what the poet William Blake might have called the 'fearful symmetry' of his music. Yet Bach himself would no doubt have said that the most important element was the last one, hard work. He seems to have been genuinely convinced that everyone else could do as well as he if they would only work hard enough. According to the composer Johann Mattheson (1681–1764) in 1739, Bach's view was that 'What I have achieved on my own by work and application, anyone else who possesses a modicum of natural talent and skill can also achieve'.[4] In a similar vein Bach's second son, Carl Philipp Emanuel, commented that 'through his own study and reflection alone he became even in his youth, a pure and strong fugue writer'.[5] Bach's first biographer, Johann Nikolaus Forkel, pointed to the same characteristic. He explained that when 'he was asked by someone, as frequently happened, for a very easy clavier piece he used to say: "I will see what I can do." In such cases, he usually chose an easy theme, but, in thoroughly working it out, always found so much of importance to say upon it that the piece could not turn out easy after all. If complaints were made that it was still too difficult, he smiled, and said "Only practise it diligently, and it will go very well; you have five just as healthy fingers on each hand as I".'[6]

Nevertheless, in subtle contradiction to the almost naive image of the devout, hard-working, rational artist whose labours are automatically rewarded, there is also another side to Bach. Mattheson went on to ask 'so I wonder why is it that there is only one master like him in the world and that no-one comes near him?' This brings us to the matter of his exceptional talent, genius, or whatever convenient word we wish to use to avoid having to explain the inexplicable. Perhaps a useful word is simply 'imagination', although Bach himself might have preferred 'invention'. He did recognize that not everybody had this, no matter how hard they worked, and that some excellent performers therefore did not have what it takes to become composers. He refused to teach composition to students incapable of 'having original musical ideas'.[7] Once an interesting basic idea was there, Bach could show a student how to develop it and build a coherent and convincing musical structure out of that idea. He could teach his own compositional techniques rationally and objectively because he had consciously developed them; but he would not waste his or the student's time by working on unimaginative musical ideas since the result would have no artistic value. He therefore recognized that he himself did have this faculty of imagination and he must have become increasingly conscious of how exceptional it was, his greatest asset, the priceless gift that not even hard work could provide.

Not everybody agrees, of course, about artistic value or imagination, although most people can agree about what is thought to be rational, logical or intelligent. The French seventeenth-century philosopher Pascal commented that the emotive heart and the rational mind are constantly at war with each other. He also noted that reason is always trying to control and dominate imagination (or, as we might say nowadays, trying to explain, define and contextualize it). Pascal concluded that in the end reason always loses because 'imagination disposes of everything, imagination creates beauty'.[8] Modern thinkers no longer write like this, yet it is revealing to approach Bach with these two concepts in mind. If the family's musical tradition and Lutheranism were the twin foundations on which he built, the one perfectly compatible with the other, then inventive imagination and rational thinking were the bricks and mortar with which he constructed his solid musical edifice, and they sprang from his own personal skills rather than from any heritage. Moreover, in contrast to the first two, they were not by nature mutually compatible and therefore set up a fruitful friction. Pascal's conclusion that 'imagination creates beauty' suggests that, for a musician of Bach's period, what struck the listener as beautiful could never be fully defined or explained. Bach would no doubt have agreed, despite all his rational approach to teaching. His works have an equilibrium between the two warring factions that is unique in the history of music.

Eisenach, Ohrdruf, Lüneburg

Surprisingly little is known about the first seventeen years of Bach's life, during which he lived in, and was educated in, Eisenach, Ohrdruf and Lüneburg. His mother, Maria Elisabetha Lämmerhirt (1644–94), came from a solid musical family well established in the region (in 1999 there were still thirteen Lämmerhirts listed in the Eisenach telephone directory). His father, Johann Ambrosius Bach (1645–95), had been a municipal musician (*Stadtpfeifer*) and violinist in the nearby town of Erfurt before settling in Eisenach as court trumpeter and director of the town's music; he was also an instrumentalist at St George's church (the Georgenkirche). A fine portrait of him survives.[9] The present *Bachhaus* museum in Eisenach cannot be identified with certainty as the house in which Johann Sebastian was born. When he was two days old, on 23 March 1685, he was baptized in St George's church (where Luther had preached in 1521), a rather splendid late medieval building. The baptismal font dating from 1503 is still there, standing at the centre of the church. Although there was a family tradition of naming the boys Johann, in fact his names came, as was then usual, from his two godfathers: Johann Georg Koch, a minor forestry official in Eisenach, and Sebastian Nagel, a municipal musician in the nearby town of Gotha. Both must have been colleagues of Johann Ambrosius.

Eisenach may have been a relatively small town but it was able to provide the boy with significant musical experiences at an early age. He presumably learnt from Johann Ambrosius the rudiments of musical notation and how to play string instruments. He could have acquired some familiarity with the organ (or at least have felt at home in the organ loft) since the organist at St George's was a relative of Johann Ambrosius, the excellent Johann Christoph Bach (1642–1703), whom Johann Sebastian later described as a '*profound* composer' and who, according to Carl Philipp Emanuel 'was strong in the invention of beautiful ideas'. Of all the earlier members of the Bach family he is certainly the most significant composer.[10] Johann Christoph was court harpsichordist to the Duke of Eisenach and had therefore been a colleague of the great Johann Pachelbel, who was court organist from May 1677 to May 1678 before moving to nearby Erfurt until 1690. Pachelbel, who was described by one of his Eisenach colleagues, Daniel Eberlin, as a 'perfect and rare virtuoso', was clearly a friend of Johann Ambrosius.[11] Their bond lasted after Pachelbel left Eisenach since in 1680 he became godfather to Bach's elder sister Johanna Juditha. (She died in 1686.) While in Erfurt Pachelbel also later taught Bach's elder brother, from 1685 to 1688. If he had not moved to Erfurt seven years before Johann Sebastian's birth, he could easily have become his godfather and perhaps teacher.

Bach went to school at the Lateinschule in Eisenach, a former Dominican monastery of which parts still exist (although the institution now bears Luther's name). He was there from spring 1692 until 1695. The school records show his frequent absences, especially during the last year, perhaps linked with the series of deaths in the family. One of his older brothers, Johann Balthasar (*b.* 1673), had died in 1691. He was soon followed by one of Johann Ambrosius's uncles, Heinrich (1615–92), organist of the Liebfrauenkirche in Arnstadt and known in his day as a fine composer of chorales, motets, concertos, prelude and fugues.[12] The following year his father's identical twin brother, Johann Christoph Bach (1645–93) also died; he had been a town musician and violinist in Eisenach. (Confusingly, this is not the same Johann Christoph who was organist at St George's in Eisenach.) Next came the turn of another of his father's cousins, Johann Michael Bach (1648–94), former organist in Arnstadt and town organist in Gehren, whose two daughters Barbara Catharina and Maria Barbara will figure later in Johann Sebastian's life, as we shall see; Johann Michael was also an excellent composer and a significant instrument-maker. Then, in close succession came the two hardest blows. In 1694, Johann Sebastian's mother, Maria Elisabetha, died at the age of 50. Johann Ambrosius remarried quickly, to Barbara Margaretha Keul, the widow of his cousin, the organist Johann Günther Bach (1653–83). And then Johann Ambrosius suddenly died too, also at the age of 50, in February 1695. It was three months after the wedding and just one month before Bach's tenth birthday. After all these deaths, it is easy to understand the wording of the formal request for help made on 4 March 1695 to the burgomaster of Eisenach by Johann Ambrosius's second wife, who now found herself a widow once again. Bach's new stepmother noted in her request for help for the 'poor fatherless and motherless orphans' that 'the dear God had caused the springs of musical talent in the Bach family to run dry within the last few years'.[13] The phrase is ironic only with the wisdom of hindsight. The word *Bach* in German means a spring or a stream. She may be forgiven for being unaware that the family's greatest stream was far from having 'run dry', and was about to open up into a great river of unprecedented abundance.[14]

And so the family was split up. Barbara Margaretha returned to Arnstadt (where her father was burgomaster), taking with her Bach's older sister Maria Salome (1677–1727). The two youngest boys, Johann Jacob (1682–1722) and Johann Sebastian, went to live in nearby Ohrdruf with their eldest brother Johann Christoph Bach (1671–1721), yet another Bach with the same name (in all, there are eight musicians with this name in the family tree). He was nearly 24 and, following his studies with Pachelbel in Erfurt, had been organist for five years at St Michael's church in Ohrdruf. Carl Philipp Emanuel mentioned some 50 years later that Bach did not start keyboard studies in Eisenach.[15] Perhaps he was simply refer-ring to organ studies since by the time Johann Sebastian left Eisenach in 1695, at the age of nine, he would still not have been tall enough for his feet to reach the pedals. The boy was fortunate in now being able rapidly to acquire solid skills as an organist under his brother's tuition. In Ohrdruf, he and Johann Jacob attended the prestigious Lyceum, a school comparable to the Eisenach Lateinschule. Johann Sebastian's intellectual capacities can be inferred from the school records; within two years he had reached the top of his class. Johann Jacob, for whom Johann Sebastian clearly retained a special affection, left after one year, at the age of fourteen. He returned to Eisenach as an apprentice to the wind player Johann Heinrich Halle, their father's successor, and went on to become a professional oboe and flute player. He travelled to Sweden and Turkey where, rather surprisingly, he took flute lessons with the illustrious French player Pierre-Gabriel Buffardin (*c.*1690–1768). Johann Sebastian later wrote in his honour the 'Capriccio on the departure of a dearly beloved brother' (*Capriccio sopra la lontananza del fratello diletissimo*, BWV 992), dating from 1704–07.

Some indication of Johann Sebastian's early musical aptitude may be understood from an anecdote, recounted some years after Bach's death. Apparently Johann Christoph had a volume of music containing pieces by the eminent organ composers Froberger, Kerll and Pachelbel. The young boy wished to study these works and therefore copied them out surreptitiously, at night and by candlelight, but the copy was soon confiscated. (Bach only got it back nearly twenty years later, after his brother's death.) Whatever the truth of the story, the document recounting this episode (the 1754 obituary, written partly by Carl Philipp Emanuel) specifically mentions Bach's 'very passion to improve himself in music and the very industry applied to the aforesaid book'.[16] Here is one of the earliest signs of Bach's ambition and his capacity for hard work, at the age of only twelve or thirteen. Although Johann Christoph seems to have been a rather severe teacher, he understood that the most urgent task was to give his youngest brother a basic education and a solid grounding in a practical trade that would enable him to become financially self-sufficient as quickly as possible. That he did this honourably may be inferred from Johann Sebastian having dedicated one of his finest early keyboard works to him, the *Capriccio in honorem Johann Christoph Bachii Ohrdrufiensis*, BWV 993.

The fact that Johann Jacob had been apprenticed at the age of fourteen suggests he may not have been as gifted intellectually as his young brother. At any rate, when it was Johann Sebastian's turn to leave the Ohrdruf Lyceum, arrangements were made for him to continue his schooling. He left a week before his fifteenth birthday, graduating on 15 March 1700. He was sent to a special school in the beautiful walled town of Lüneburg, outside the family's home region of Thuringia and just south of Hamburg, a long way to the north. He arrived there just over two weeks later. The connection was probably provided by the cantor at Ohrdruf, Elias Herda, who had also been trained at Lüneburg. Bach stayed there for two years. Since his voice was unusually good, he became a member of the matins choir (Mettenchor) of St Michael's church (the Michaeliskirche, founded in 955) which, according to an old decree, was open to 'children of poor parents, who have nothing to live on but have good treble voices'.[17] A painting survives of the interior, by Joachim Burmester and dating from soon after 1700.[18] It shows a spacious building and an impressive, large organ on the north wall. (This instrument was given a major rebuild three years after Bach left.) Bach was given a free education at St Michael's school (the Michaelisschule, founded in 1430, also referred to as the Michaels-Gymnasium), the less socially distinguished of the church's two schools (the other being the Ritterakademie, for sons of the nobility). The school still exists and a fascinating catalogue of its music library survives, made in 1695, just before Bach's arrival. It indicates the sort of repertoire he would have sung. (The 1100 titles include works by Monteverdi, Grandi, Carissimi, Casati, Rosenmüller, Schütz – 30 works, Capricornus, Schelle and Knüpfer, as well as a now lost large-scale choral work by Pachelbel based on the Lutheran chorale 'Wenn wir in höchsten Nöten sein', a tune of which Bach appears to have been particularly fond right to the end of his life.)[19] The boys in the choir could earn some money through their musical performances. Bach had been able to enter the school because he still had his boy's treble voice. When it finally broke, he apparently spoke and sang in octaves for a whole week, before 'he lost his soprano tones and with them his fine voice'.[20]

In Lüneburg his musical horizons were greatly broadened. It must always have been his idea that he should become an organist in one of the Thuringian churches so his prime energies were now devoted to deepening his knowledge of organ building and repairing, developing his skills in organ playing and increasing his understanding of the various different styles of composing for the instrument. Through his brother he had already become fully familiar with the south German tradition of Pachelbel (identifiable in his earliest works, such as the chorales in the Neumeister collection in Yale, first published in 1985). He was now close to several of the greatest organists in northern Germany, the style of whose music was quite different. Notable among them was Georg Böhm (1661–1733) who had been born near Ohrdruf and was probably trained by members of the Bach dynasty in Goldbach and Gotha. He would have considered Bach a 'fellow countryman'. In 1698 he had been appointed organist of St John's church in Lüneburg. The organ was even more impressive and certainly more modern than that in St Michael's church. According to Carl Philipp Emanuel, Johann Sebastian 'loved and studied' Böhm's works.[21] Some of them, such as the remarkable organ setting of the chorale 'Vater unser im Himmelsreich', could have provided a model for him. Their intensely emotional and personal musical language is partly indebted to the ornamental techniques of the great French organists of the seventeenth century. Nothing in Pachelbel's music had prepared Johann Sebastian for this. It was a style that he adopted – and adapted – and to which he remained faithful all his life. Böhm clearly remained in contact with Bach since his address is mentioned in a newspaper article announcing the publication in 1727 of Bach's first two harpsichord partitas, BWV 825 and 826. Copies are said to be available 'at the house of Monsieur Boehm, organist of St John's church, Lüneburg'.[22]

Apart from his activities in Lüneburg, there was also the much richer and more varied musical life in nearby Hamburg. We do not know how, if at all, Bach participated in it, but he surely cannot have been unaware of it. He is reported to have undertaken the journey 'fairly frequently' (on foot) in order to hear the best organs and organ playing. Perhaps he also attended other concerts. Every Sunday throughout the winter 1700–01, a series of concerts was organized by the imperial ambassador and Holy Roman plenipotentiary in Hamburg, Count von Eckgh, under the artistic direction of Reinhard Keiser (1674–1739) or Johann Mattheson, who were not much older than Bach himself. And twelve operas by Keiser were produced in Hamburg between 1700 and 1702.[23] Bach could have first heard here the new Italian style of singing, which Mattheson admits having first learned in Hamburg.

Nevertheless, the main influences at this time centred on the organ. Bach came into contact with the wonderful instruments of the great organ builder Arp Schnitger (1648–1719) whose workshop was in nearby Neuenfelde. He built nearly twenty fine instruments in the area, some of the finest of which were in Hamburg. The best was considered to be the one in the Nicolaikirche, built in 1682–7, with four manuals and 62 stops; it was later described by Mattheson as an 'extraordinary organ'. The instrument in the Jacobikirche was built in 1689–93; Bach later applied for the organist's post here, in 1720. But he was also certainly aware of the four-manual organ with 58 stops in the Catharinenkirche, famous for its 16-foot reed stops. Its magnificent 32-foot principal pipes and the pedal trumpet were specifically praised by him at a later date.[24] The organist there was Johann Adam Reincken (1623–1722), a pupil of the famous Heinrich Scheidemann (c.1595–1663), who had himself been a pupil of the even more eminent Jan Pieterszoon Sweelinck (1562–1621) in Amsterdam. Reincken was a renowned concert organist and probably taught Georg Böhm. One of Bach's tributes to him may be seen in the arrangements for keyboard that he made of movements from three string sonatas first published in 1687 (BWV 954, 965 and 966); another may be the great Fantasia and Fugue in G minor for organ, BWV 542.

Bach had arrived in Lüneburg with a musical lineage that linked him in a direct student-to-teacher line to one of the greatest figures of German organ music: J. S. Bach – Johann Christoph Bach – Pachelbel. By the time he left Lüneburg, he would have been conscious of an even more distinguished direct line of pupils and teachers linking him back across 100 years to the legendary 'maker of organists' in Amsterdam: J. S. Bach – Böhm – Reincken – Scheidemann – Sweelinck, an artistic lineage that outweighed his own family tradition. He had drawn everything possible from his family's disciplined South German tradition. Now, at the age of seventeen, he had also already understood what could be learnt from the finest masters of the more imaginative north German tradition, even if he had not yet quite digested it. The one missing element was a contact with Dietrich Buxtehude, the great organist of Lübeck, further to the north. As we shall see, Bach repaired this omission in 1705. So here again are the twin forces of rational discipline and imaginative freedom which combine in Bach, this time as the result of two separate organ schools. The fact that he did not now go to Nuremberg to study with Pachelbel suggests that he was already more attracted to the northern tradition. Many of his earliest pieces, in common with the finest works of the northern school, are written in the 'fantastic' style, alternating improvisatory passages with learned fugues, and then interrupting these with astonishing dissonances. These characteristics all help to give organ works of this school an unprecedented dramatic force and rhetorical effect where, indeed, 'imagination creates beauty'.

All the components of Bach's character were in place by the time he left Lüneburg. It is tempting to trace the roots of his adult personality and of his lifelong habit of hard work to the difficulties of his first seventeen years. He had an absolute necessity of improving his circumstances and the only person he could rely on to do that was himself. His self-reliance, allied with his natural musical curiosity, led him to continue to learn from other composers' music and to keep improving his own compositions. He was never satisfied. In a telling comment, Forkel explains that Bach regularly revised his keyboard works 'to make, little by little, the faulty good, the good better, and the better perfect.'[25] Enormous patience was clearly a strong characteristic, at least where his own work was concerned.

Clearly, however, impatience was also part of his personality, and it can be seen from his youth. He did not suffer fools gladly and was quick to respond if he felt he was not being treated correctly, or with due dignity. One early story illustrates this rather intransigent side to his character. When he was twenty, he was struck on the face one evening in the street by a young man called Geyersbach who said that Bach had insulted him, or had at least insulted his bassoon. (Apparently Bach had said it sounded like a nanny goat, one of the earliest signs of his sense of humour.) Some fellow students of the bassoon player intervened just as Bach had drawn his sword. Bach and Geyersbach were both formally reprimanded by the authorities, but let off with a warning.[26] Many years later, a clear glimpse into this side of his character is provided by one of his few letters. It is dated 20 March 1748, the day before his 63rd birthday. The chilling tone confirms that Bach was not a man to be trifled with. The poor recipient of his ire had apparently not delivered or returned an instrument on time:

> Mr Martius,
> My patience has reached its limit. How long do you think I will wait for the harpsichord? Two months have already gone by and nothing has changed. I regret having to write to you in this manner, but I have no choice. You should put things right within five days from now, or we shall never be good friends.
> Adieu. Joh. Sebast. Bach.[27]

One can almost hear him getting his sword ready again. With a character like this, it is not surprising that in later life some of his colleagues found him difficult or that he was frequently in conflict with those who had authority over him.

He was not always an easy man to get on with and he sometimes appears to be rather irascible. Yet among the many stories that are told about him very few show him up as a schemer, and none as someone who ever tried to take advantage of others. Yet he was not above pressing his own advantage whenever he could. He knew how to manipulate his employers, like many ambitious and talented people. He had an earthy sense of humour, and his pupils attest to his generosity. Like all great men, he had 'strong weaknesses'. It is precisely because they were so striking that they help us to see him in a very human light.

'Ein starker Appetit...'

'A keen appetite'. Stories about food arise at various moments in Bach's life, and the portraits suggest someone who liked to eat well. Some of these stories are capricious, others amusing; a few are probably legendary. Occasionally, even a tiny incident can provide a refreshing glimpse into more normal, everyday aspects of his life. The first such episode took place in about 1701–02.

He was at school in Lüneburg – near Hamburg, where at the time a very able organist and composer, named Reinecke [Reincken], was in his prime. Since he made several trips to see this master, it happened one day, since he stayed longer in Hamburg than the state of his purse permitted, that on his way home to Lüneburg he had only a couple of schillings in his pocket. He had not got half way home yet when he developed a keen appetite and accordingly went into an inn, where the savoury odours from the kitchen only made the state in which he found himself ten times more painful. In the midst of his sad meditations on this subject, he heard the grinding noise of a window opening and saw a pair of herring heads thrown out onto the rubbish pile. Since he was a true Thuringian, the sight of these heads made his mouth begin to water, and he lost not a second in taking possession of them. And lo and behold! he had hardly started to tear them apart when he found a Danish ducat hidden in each head. This find enabled him not only to add a portion of roast meat to his meal but also at the first opportunity to make another pilgrimage, in greater comfort, to Mr Reinecke in Hamburg. It is remarkable that the unknown benefactor, who must undoubtedly have watched from the window to see who would be lucky enough to find his gift, did not have the curiosity to ascertain more closely the identity and personality of the finder.

Friedrich Wilhelm Marpurg, 1786[1]

In June 1707, when Bach was appointed organist in Mühlhausen, part of his yearly salary was to include 54 bushels of grain.[2] The next year, at Weimar, his salary was fixed as including only 30 bushels but, as we shall see, he had other advantages of a more liquid variety.[3]

Nearly ten years later, in late April 1716, Bach visited Halle to test the new organ in the Liebfrauenkirche, which had taken nearly four years to build, at a cost of 6,300 thalers. He was the junior member of a group of three experts, his senior colleagues being Johann Kuhnau (1660–1722) and Christian Friedrich Rolle (1681–1751). For three days they examined the three-manual instrument and all of its 65 stops, testing the wind supply, checking the metal content of the alloy pipes, verifying the wind pressure, the weight of the keys in the keyboards, and the quality of the tuning. Their report was rather critical in several important details and must have terrified the organ builder, Christoff Cuncius (1676–1722). The events came to a climax with a solemn sermon and a fine concert on Saturday 1 May, at which Bach no doubt played. On Sunday 2 May he received payment for his travel expenses.[4] The festivities closed with a splendid dinner the next day. The menu survives.[5]

Menu of the Dinner
of the most Worshipful Council of the Churches
on the Occasion of
the Dedication of the New Organ
—

1 piece of *Bäffallemote* (boeuf à la mode)
Pike with an anchovy butter sauce
1 smoked ham
1 dish of peas
1 dish of potatoes
2 dishes of spinach and chicory
1 roast quarter of mutton – Warm asparagus salad

Boiled pumpkin – Lettuce
Fritters – Radishes
Preserved lemon rind – Fresh butter
Preserved cherries – Roast veal

Several of Bach's cantata texts use food imagery to great effect, including various references to the miracle of multiplying the loaves and fishes. Maybe this reminded him of the 'pair of herring heads thrown out onto the rubbish pile' when he was young.

Ach! ich sehe, itzt, da ich zur Hochzeit gehe, *BWV 162, was written one year before the organ dinner (for performance on 3 November 1715). The text is by Salomo Franck. The imagery throughout is based on food, and on the image of the soul invited to the wedding feast. 'The feast is spread, the fatted calf has been killed, the preparations are magnificent...Happy is he who is invited by faith; sorry is he who disdains this feast!' The music is particularly joyous.*

Some years later he again wrote a cantata that relies heavily on food imagery, Brich dem Hungrigen dein Brot, *BWV 39 (composed for 23 June 1726). Its anonymous text, drawn partly from Isaiah, opens with the words 'Distribute your bread to the hungry'. In the magnificent instrumental introduction, pairs of chords are distributed among the instruments in systematic fashion, first to the flutes, then the oboes, then the strings, in an amusing illustration of the words. The text of the whole cantata is about receiving and giving food, heavenly and earthly.*

Bach seems to have received numerous gifts of earthly food. On one occasion, writing from Leipzig in July 1741, he thanked Jean Leberecht Schneider, Consulent *in the Chamber of finances of the Duke of Weissenfels (a court with which he had had links for over 30 years, and which had some twelve years earlier granted him the honorary title of court capellmeister). The present received had been some roast venison. The language of thanks is covered with a rich rhetorical sauce, worthy of such meat.*

Most noble Sir, Most Particularly Highly Esteemed Sir Consulent,

Although of Your Honour's invaluable favour I never entertained the slightest doubt, yet Your Honour recently deigned most graciously to give me another proof of it. I and my whole household acknowledge the same with most obedient thanks, and wish only for an opportunity to prove our desire to thank Your Honour in deeds. The fine roast venison has been, in the meantime, consumed by us, with a wish for Your Honour's good health, but we should have enjoyed it still more if we could have done so in Your Honour's agreeable compagnie. *Since, however, our wish was not fulfilled this time, we hope at least that we shall in the near future have the privilege of seeing Your Honour here with us in Leipzig, remaining, with most obedient respects to Your Most Worthy Mamma, and with proper esteem, ever,*

Your Honour's and Mr Most Particularly Highly Esteemed Sir Consulent'*s, most obedient servant,*

Joh. Seb. Bach[6]

But heavenly feasts and earthly venison were not everyday fare. Bach's family must have normally eaten simpler food. Indeed, he incorporated a popular tune about vegetables in the last of the 'Goldberg' Variations. This will be a surprise only to readers who have not yet understood that Bach had a sense of humour.

Variation 30, the Quodlibet, has two popular melodies incorporated over the unifying bass line that links all the variations. The first is an amusing little courting song: 'For a long time now I have been far from you'. The second is equally amusing, but more down to earth: 'Cabbage and beetroot have driven me away; if my mother had cooked meat, I would have remained longer!'

CHAPTER TWO

Organist and Court Composer
(1703–1717)

There is nothing remarkable about it. All one has to do is hit the right notes at the right time and the instrument plays itself.

Bach, on his own organ playing, according to J. F. Köhler, c.1776[1]

Bach's first appointment rapidly turned to a disappointment, literally. In late 1702, at the age of seventeen, he was accepted as organist at St James's church (the Jacobikirche) in Sangerhausen, as successor to Gottfried Christoph Gräffenhayn, who had died in early July. The church council voted unanimously for Bach. However, Duke Johann Georg of Saxe-Weissenfels intervened on behalf of one of his employees, Johann Augustin Kobelius (1674–1731), who had studied in Venice, was older, and perhaps appeared to be the more experienced candidate. As a result, Kobelius was appointed instead, in November 1702.

Bach was now eighteen. It is worth stopping a moment to consider how extensive his training had already been. He had become thoroughly familiar with the most important aspects of both the northern and the southern German styles of playing and composing for the organ (and presumably with other kinds of church music as well). In Hamburg he would have heard different styles of music, strongly influenced by secular Italian styles of composing and of singing. In Lüneburg he had acquired a deeper understanding of the other great musical style of the period, associated with the French court dances. The dancing master at the Ritterakademie there had been a French musician, Thomas de la

Selle, who also played in nearby Celle, where Duke Georg Wilhelm of Braunschweig-Lüneburg and his witty French wife, Eleonore Desmier d'Olbreuse, had an orchestra made up largely of French or French-trained players. Apparently Bach often went to hear these musicians play.[2] This must certainly have helped deepen his understanding not only of the French styles of composing (which he could learn from studying the scores of French music) but also, equally important, of the particular French manner of performing. This was difficult to learn on paper since many features were not fully notated in the scores and the skill was not widely shared in Germany at that time.

A document dated 4 March 1703 refers to him as *Lagueij* (*Laquey*) at the court of Duke Johann Ernst of Saxe-Weimar (1664–1707), the younger brother of the reigning duke, Wilhelm Ernst.[3] Weimar was a little town with one big castle and two little ones. Bach therefore worked in one of the two lesser princely residences, separated by an all-important covered bridge from the principal castle.[4] He seems to have worked as a violinist and the post was clearly a stop-gap for a few months. Another reference dated 1703 refers to him as 'Court Organist' in Weimar,[5] implying that he sometimes deputized for Johann Effler, the court organist.

During these months, however, Johann Sebastian Bach was biding his time, waiting for another suitable organist's post to come up. He did not have to wait long.

Arnstadt

Bach now benefited from a situation comparable to the one that had deprived him of the post in Sangerhausen. A new organ had been built in Arnstadt by Johann Friedrich Wender of Mühlhausen, and had been installed in the 'third church' or New Church (Neukirche) between 1699 and 1703. The console of this two-manual instrument still survives.[6] A new organist, a certain Andreas Börner (1673–1728), was officially appointed, but Bach was a member of the committee that examined the organ for approval and it was he who played the opening concert in late June or early July 1703. On 13 July 1703 he was paid his fee and reimbursed for his expenses (which included the hiring of horses), all paid out of the city's tax on beer.[7] Some behind-the-scenes intriguing must have then gone on since on 9 August 1703, Börner was ejected from his appointment as unceremoniously as Bach had been in Sangerhausen.[8] The post was offered to Bach and he accepted on 14 August. His salary was 50 florins, plus 30 florins for board and lodging. These 80 florins were to be paid as follows: 25 from the church funds; 25 from the city's beer taxes; and 30 from the funds of the hospital of St George and St James, where Bach may also have been expected to play the organ occasionally for services. This salary was rather high for such a post and reflects a recognition of his superior skills, despite being only eighteen years old. The earliest signed document we have from his hand, dated 28 September 1703, is a receipt for salary relating to his first few weeks' work.[9]

The Bach family had long had strong links with Arnstadt. The name Bach must have been virtually synonymous with 'musician' for nearly a century. Five musicians from another branch of the family are known to have lived there in the seventeenth century. Caspar Bach (c.1570–c.1640) had been a town bassoonist from 1620 onwards. Three of his sons were employed as municipal musicians: Melchior (1603–34), Nicolaus (1618–37) and Johannes (1602–32). A fourth son, the blind musician Heinrich Bach, had died there in 1635. However, Johann Sebastian's real links with Arnstadt went back 50 years, to the time when his grandfather moved there. Christoph Bach (1613–61), Johann Ambrosius's father, had become a town musician in 1654, probably partly because his younger brother, Heinrich, was already there and had been organist at the Liebfrauenkirche from 1641. Heinrich's son, Johann Günther Bach (1653–83), had been assistant organist and, by a curious twist of the family tree, was the first husband of Barbara Margaretha Keul. Christoph's son, Johann Christoph, had been a town musician from 1671 until his death. Johann Christoph's twin brother, Johann Ambrosius Bach, had himself been a *Stadtpfeifer* in Arnstadt until 1667; Barbara Margaretha Keul became his second wife, and Johann Sebastian's stepmother, in 1694.

The musical establishment of the town was so closely interconnected that Andreas Börner, the organist whom Bach had displaced, was linked to the Bach family: his wife at this time was Maria Elisabeth Herthum, daughter of Maria Catharina Bach

(1651–87), who had the same grandfather as Johann Ambrosius Bach. Börner's wife was thus a distant cousin of Johann Sebastian.[10]

Although by 1704 all these illustrious men of the Bach family were dead, several of the wives and daughters were still alive. Bach's return to Arnstadt must have had as much to do with the living family members as with the illustrious dead. Given these links, it is not surprising that Barbara Margaretha returned there in 1695, following Johann Ambrosius's untimely death, three months after their marriage. She took with her Bach's sister, Maria Salome. Johann Christoph's widow, Bach's aunt Martha Elisabetha Eisentraut, still lived there (she died only in 1719); that Bach remained in close contact with her is shown by the fact that their son, the organist Johann Ernst Bach (1683–1739) succeeded Bach in the post at the New Church when he left four years later. Arnstadt's claim to be the most important city for the Bach dynasty is supported by the fact that at least 24 members of the family are known to have been buried in the old cemetery.[11]

Bach's four years in Arnstadt provided him with plenty of opportunity to develop his organ technique without direct guidance, limited only by his own hard work, intelligence and imagination. He was also free to experiment in various styles of organ composition. This must have been a great period of personal development. Although he had now finished his formal studies, nevertheless he did not consider his training to be over. Freed from direct contact with a teacher, he assumed entirely the responsibility for continuing to train himself, not just as a player but as a composer. Carl Philipp Emanuel commented after Johann Sebastian's death that in Arnstadt 'he really showed the first fruits of his application to the art of organ playing, and to composition, which he had chiefly learned by the observation of the works of the most famous and proficient composers of his day and by the fruits of his own reflection upon them'.[12]

It is touching to sense him, two years later, no doubt after a period of more prolonged private work, more intense than at any stage in his life up until then, apparently feeling the need for a final contact with one of the established masters. It is as if he were seeking final confirmation that his training period was really over. At the age of twenty, he decided to return to the north to visit Buxtehude, generally considered to be the greatest organist in

Germany and an exceptionally fine composer of cantatas and chamber music. Pachelbel himself had recently dedicated to Buxtehude his published keyboard collection *Hexachordum Apollinis, Sex Arias exhibens* (November 1699) and planned to send his own son to study with him.[13]

The visit to Lübeck

Bach may already have come into contact with Dietrich Buxtehude (*c*.1637–1707) in Hamburg. The fact that the older man, on his side, was seeking a successor as organist of the Marienkirche, a splendid twin-towered church right in the middle of the town, may well have been an added incentive. Bach all his life showed an awareness of potential job opportunities, although many of them did not work out.

When Buxtehude obtained the Lübeck post in 1668, he had married the daughter of his illustrious predecessor, Franz Tunder (1614–67). He now expected the same to happen again since he had an unmarried daughter, Anna Margareta. Both Handel and Mattheson had already visited together in August 1703 (composing 'numerous double fugues in the carriage'),[14] but they had returned to Hamburg still unmarried. (Mattheson married the daughter of an English minister in 1709. Handel, of course, never married; a recent article by Gary C. Thomas fills in the context.)[15] Bach was also still unmarried. He asked for a month's leave of absence and arranged for a deputy to play for him. He left Arnstadt in late October 1705.

Unlike Handel and Mattheson, he could not afford to take a carriage and had to make the very considerable journey on foot, so it is unlikely that he arrived in Lübeck before early November. Like Handel and Mattheson, on the other hand, Bach eventually returned home. It is hard to imagine he was not interested in the post. And even harder to imagine that Buxtehude was not impressed by his abilities. We must conclude that one of the reasons for his return may have been that, like Mattheson and Handel, he was unwilling to marry Anna Margareta Buxtehude. At 30, she was considerably older than all three young postulants. A few months after Bach left, Buxtehude appointed the organist

Johann Christian Schieferdecker (1679–1732) to be his assistant. In 1707 he duly married Anna Margareta.[16]

Johann Sebastian had perhaps already been planning to marry someone else since, while in Arnstadt, he had become more closely acquainted with his second cousin, Maria Barbara Bach. She was the daughter of his relative Johann Michael Bach (their grandfathers were brothers). Maria Barbara was five months older than Johann Sebastian, having been born on 20 October 1684, in Arnstadt. However, his financial situation does not appear to have been sufficiently stable to allow them to marry yet.

Bach stayed in Lübeck four months, much longer than Handel and Mattheson, who seem to have spent only one day there before taking their carriage back to Hamburg. He cannot have failed to be impressed by the exceptionally fine organ and in particular by the amazing battery of reed stops. According to Mattheson, writing in 1721, there were no less than fifteen separate reeds, evenly distributed across the three manuals and pedals and ranging from the very low 32' pitch up to exceptionally high and rare 2' pitch (these last two both being on the pedals).[17]

Bach's decision to stay on for a few months allowed him to attend not only the famous concerts of 'evening music' (*Abend-Musik*) that Buxtehude presented in the Marienkirche in December, on three Sundays during the Advent season, but also the extra musical festivities associated with Christmas and the New Year. Moreover, Buxtehude had composed some particularly elaborate pieces in contrasting styles for ceremonies on 2–3 December 1705: *Castrum doloris*, mourning music to mark the death of the Emperor Leopold I; and *Templum honoris*, a celebratory work to mark the accession of Joseph I.[18]

As great a man as Buxtehude cannot have failed to realize that this young man was the most brilliant organist he had ever encountered. It is likely to have been one of those occasions when an ageing master understands (perhaps silently) that he has met someone who is destined to surpass him. Yet Bach, on his side, had gone to Lübeck in order to hear Buxtehude play the organ. He must have been overwhelmed by the older man's playing, a model of imaginative, surprising, improvisatory strength, wonderfully channelled by intellectual control and long experience into larger musical structures that were held in place by learned counterpoint.

This was music in one of its most compelling guises: art that disguises its artistry (which is the composer's business and, to a lesser extent, the performer's) yet fully reveals its emotional expressiveness (which is the listener's business).

Yet Buxtehude was not simply an organist. He was an example in other areas also; 128 of his sacred works (cantatas and motets) survive, although certainly many others were written which are now lost. When Bach heard him he had recently published two volumes of chamber music in Hamburg, comprising fourteen excellent sonatas for violin, bass viol and harpsichord (1694, 1696).[19] No doubt the two men also discussed the more abstract and learned aspects of counterpoint. Bach would have found on Buxtehude's shelves copies of the works the older man had published following the death of his father, Johann Buxtehude, in 1674.[20] This moving little collection contains two pieces that bear the rather solemn yet modest Latin title *Contrapunctus* (simply 'counterpoint'). They are written in D minor and are examples of one of the most difficult kinds of composition, known as 'quadruple counterpoint' in mirror form. Bach returned to this idea nearly 50 years later for his own last work, *The Art of Fugue*, BWV 1080. Carl Philipp Emanuel summed up his father's visit to Buxtehude in a fine understatement: 'He tarried there, not without profit.'[21]

In October 1705, Bach had asked for one month's leave from Arnstadt, but returned home from Lübeck only in February 1706. He was formally reprimanded on 21 February and interrogated as to why he had stayed so long. His replies are recorded in the Arnstadt archives. They are disdainful, almost monosyllabic, apart from one withering comment that rings out as both dismissive and proud: he had stayed away because he had been there 'in order to comprend one thing and another about his art.'[22] But this would hardly do as an answer to his employers. The Arnstadt authorities had him in their hands and now took the opportunity to confront him with other complaints as well. Why did Bach refuse to make music with the students? Since we know that one of these seems to have been the 'nanny goat' bassoonist Geyersbach, it would appear that Bach had indeed tried, but judged them to be too feeble to waste his time with them. However, he did not now say this in reply, but simply asked the authorities constructively to appoint a real director of music.

Their most striking complaint, however, is that Bach's organ playing was not satisfactory. When accompanying the congregational chorales, he now introduced strange *variationes* (probably cadenza-like flourishes, as interludes between the lines) and played 'strange tones' (unusual chromatic harmonies), all of which disturbed the faithful. A surviving early composition fits this description perfectly: the little chorale 'Allein Gott in der Höh' sei Ehr'', BWV 715.

We should not dismiss such complaints too rapidly. Bach's chorales are less rarely used now in church for congregational singing but they have had a long, and perhaps more influential, second career as models for teaching harmony to music students. The dismay of the Arnstadt authorities at Bach's over-zealous pursuit of musical elaboration was recently echoed in a comparable attack by a modern scholar questioning the traditional dominance of Bach's chorale-settings in the harmony classroom. Philip Brett commented in 1994 on the 'questionable operations by the master upon a set of simple, defenceless tunes, rendered all but unrecognizable by the often excessive harmonic detail forced upon them.'[23]

The Arnstadt complaints nevertheless make rather painful reading. The worthy councillors, who had clearly never taken a harmony lesson in their lives, tried to tell Johann Sebastian Bach, freshly back from Lübeck after the most exciting and stimulating professional encounter of his life, how to compose music. And although they went into detail, attempting to display their knowledge, in fact they only showed their ignorance of even the rudiments of musical theory and terminology. Their last complaint was that whereas he had already been reprimanded for playing preludes that were too long, now he had immediately gone to the 'extreme opposite' and was playing preludes that were much too short!

The writing was on the wall. It is easy to see why the authorities were so irritated by Bach's attitude, which must have seemed arrogant, especially in someone so young. But is it any more difficult to understand why Bach's replies were non-communicative to the point of being discourteous? Clearly he thought that the people he was talking to would not be capable of understanding the 'one thing and another about his art' that he had just learnt, even if he explained in detail.

The situation in Arnstadt deteriorated further over the following months and by November 1706 other complaints were made: that he still refused to play with the students (Bach prevaricated, saying that he would reply to the charge in writing); and that he had even allowed an 'unfamiliar maiden to be invited into the choir loft and let her make music there' (to which Bach curtly replied that he had already explained this to one of the council).[24] It is not known who this was, but she is likely to have been a family member. The favoured candidate, not surprisingly, has always been his cousin Maria Barbara.

Bach was now unhappy in his post, was working for people who did not understand him, had incompetent musical colleagues and wanted to get married but could not do so. After four years in Arnstadt, it was time to move.

Mühlhausen and marriage to Maria Barbara

The opportunity to move arose three weeks after his last reprimand, on the death of the organist at St Blasius, the principal parish church in the old town in nearby Mühlhausen. Candidates were invited to apply. Bach went to play, on trial, on Easter Sunday (24 April 1707) and may also have produced his cantata *Christ lag in Todes Banden*, BWV 4. It is a wonderful work, in the intimate but profound style of Buxtehude. Some of the other candidates withdrew, astutely realizing that they had little chance.[25] By the time the authorities came to vote on 24 May, there was only one candidate left. Bach was interviewed formally on 14 June. His salary was fixed as 'the same as he had received in Arnstadt'. However, he pressed his advantage by also asking for 54 bushels of grain, some wood and 360 faggots, all to be 'delivered to his door'. His terms were accepted and he was appointed unanimously on 15 June 1707. The agreement was sealed with a handshake.[26]

The last important thing he did in Arnstadt was to marry Maria Barbara, not because he was still employed there but because it was her home town and that of her family. On 10 August 1707 his mother's uncle, Tobias Lämmerhirt, had died and left Johann Sebastian the substantial sum of 50 *gulden*, more than half his annual salary. This allowed him to set up his own house. He and

Maria Barbara were married in Dornheim (just to the east of Arnstadt) on 17 October 1707. The pastor of the church, J. L. Stauber, was one of the family.[27]

In Mühlhausen, things seem to have started well. Bach had moved up from being organist at a 'third church' to being municipal organist in the principal church, responsible directly to the two burgomasters. A few months later, on 4 February 1708, he was able to publish his first work, a 'Festive Church Motetto' now known as the cantata 'God is my king', *Gott ist mein König*, BWV 71. Although the title might suggest that this is a sacred work, it was in fact composed to celebrate the inauguration of the town council. The whole affair was really a civic ceremony. It was performed in St Mary's church in the new town (not at St Blasius in the old town, where Bach was organist). The text is addressed to the new emperor, Joseph I, not to God. The title of the cantata does not appear on the title-page of the publication, so God is not even mentioned. Bach's name is printed very small. By far the largest-size type is reserved for the names of the two 'Most Deserving Burgomasters', Adolf Strecker and Georg Adam Steinbach, who no doubt paid for the printing.[28]

During the next couple of weeks, Bach decided to take immediate advantage of his success and drew up detailed instructions for improving the organ, which dated from the sixteenth century but had been rebuilt by the local builder J. F. Wender (with whom Bach had already worked in Arnstadt). His plans for an enlarged instrument with three manuals and pedals were approved on 21 February. The new organ was to be more varied than the one in Arnstadt and have a particularly colourful range of stops.[29]

Nevertheless, he resigned four months later, on 25 June 1708. His resignation letter survives.[30] After explaining how happy he had been to come to Mühlhausen and how grateful he was for having been given the opportunity to improve the music in the church, he comments that he has nevertheless been able to change little, adding 'No matter how simply I live, I remain poor, considering the house rent and other most necessary expenses.' More to the point, the Duke of Weimar had offered him a better post. Bach rather loftily explains 'I have received the gracious admission of His Serene Highness of Saxe-Weimar into his Court Chapel and Chamber Music.' His previous appointment in Weimar, five years earlier, had been at the

Interior of the palace church (*Himmelsburg*) at Weimar, site of Bach's cantata performances, with organ loft cut in the ceiling. Gouache by Christian Richter (*d.* 1667), *c.*1660.

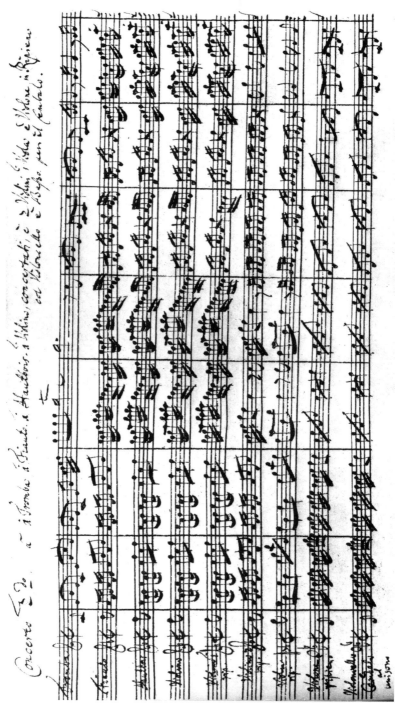

Autograph score of the beginning of the first movement of the Brandenburg Concerto No. 2 in F major, BWV 1047, probably written in Cöthen 1717–18.

Autograph score of the first movement of the Sonata in G minor for solo violin, BWV 1001, Cöthen 1720.

'Still-life with Smoking Utensils' by Jean Baptiste Simeon Chardin (1699–1779), *c.*1760–63. Oil on canvas.

Engraving of the St Thomaskirche and Thomasschule, Leipzig, by Johann Gottfried Krügner (1684–1769), dated 1723.

lesser of the two courts, that of Duke Johann Ernst, who had since died (in 1707). The new post was at the more important court of his elder brother, the reigning duke, Wilhelm Ernst (1662–1728). Bach would thus work in the main castle and become not merely organist in the chapel but also one of the court chamber musicians.

The authorities in Mühlhausen accepted his resignation the next day, 26 June, since they could hardly oppose the wishes of the duke, and Bach, with his stubborn character, had evidently made up his mind to leave. They were resigned to their fate, noting with a certain lucidity that 'since he could not be made to stay, consent must doubtless be given to his dismissal'.[31] Moreover, although they knew they had a good man, Bach had met with some real opposition from a group of the parishioners, to which he tactfully alludes in his letter. He was asked to continue to oversee the rebuilding of the organ that he had set in motion.

Weimar and the visit to Halle

The previous court organist in Weimar was Johann Effler, for whom Bach had already deputized in 1703. Effler had formerly been organist in Gehren, where he had been succeeded by Johann Michael Bach, the father of Johann Sebastian's new wife.[32] Once again, we can see that although Bach's talent always made him stand out, his family connections were helping him. Effler was now 'old and sick'. He was pensioned off gracefully on his full salary, 130 florins, to make way for his brilliant young replacement who, at the age of 23, was nevertheless granted a salary of 150 florins. According to the duke's decree, dated 20 July 1708, Bach was also to receive 18 bushels of corn, 12 bushels of barley, a substantial amount of wood, and 30 buckets of beer from the castle's brewery.[33]

The old family network may have helped in another way also. A former musician at the court of Weimar, Adam Drese (c.1620–1701), had lived in Arnstadt for the last twenty years of his life and had been a colleague of various members of the Bach dynasty. He had a fine reputation as a teacher. (Better, perhaps, than his reputation as a composer: following an unsuccessful opera composed in 1676, *Adam and Eve* – a rather odd subject for an opera – his 'sacred comedy' on the resurrection of Christ, performed in 1677 by the students of the University of Jena, had caused a scandal.)[34] When Bach arrived in Weimar he became a junior colleague of Adam Drese's nephew and student, Johann Samuel (Salomo) Drese (1644–1716), who had been *Capellmeister* since before Bach was born. He was now old and infirm.

Bach started taking on most of the duties of *Capellmeister* from 1714 until Drese's death two years later. By special decree of the duke on 20 March 1715, the day before his 30th birthday, Bach was entitled to receive the same honorarium payments as a *Capellmeister*, but without having the title.[35] (And he did not thereby acquire the *Capellmeister*'s right to receive every day one measure of beer from the castle cellars and one small loaf.)[36] Johann Samuel's son, Johann Wilhelm Drese (1677–1745), held the title of vice-*Capellmeister* and received similar extra payments, but his main talent was being the son of his father. So although Bach's dynastic connections had helped him to get the Weimar job, he arrived in a place where another little dynasty was already in the key positions. Here were the seeds of trouble.

Bach's social standing had considerably increased. Instead of being municipal organist of a parish church, he was now court organist at the principal castle, a fine building dating from 1658 and known colloquially as *Wilhelmsburg* (Williamstown). The chapel, in the south-eastern part of the castle, was known as *Himmelsburg* (Heavenstown).[37] His salary had increased and in 1711 it shot up by over 30 per cent, to 200 florins. When he was also named to the post of *Conzertmeister* in 1714, there was a further increase and yet another one in 1715. By the time he left Weimar in 1717, his salary had reached 250 florins.[38] In addition, there were numerous other extras such as money for coal during the winter and he was granted a much larger allowance of wood than he had received in Mühlhausen, perhaps because of the geographical position of Weimar closer to the Thuringian forest.

His teaching also brought in more cash and he was paid for playing organ concerts as well as for examining new organs. Although through his position of organist he depended directly on the reigning duke, Wilhelm Ernst, the presence in Weimar of two reigning families meant that Bach was formally considered as one of the 'joint servants' (*gemeinschaftlichen Dienern*) of both ducal families. This situation contained more seeds of trouble.

Every year, he also received a gift of two florins from Duke Wilhelm Ernst on his name-day, the feast of St William. Bach was not the only musician to receive this, but it does draw attention to the fact that the duke had been personally impressed by his playing and took a direct interest in the new organist. Carl Philipp Emanuel comments that the pleasure the duke took in Bach's playing 'fired him with the desire to try out every possible artistry in his treatment of the organ' and notes that most of Bach's organ works were composed in Weimar.[39] The findings of modern scholarship support this comment. Over 230 organ works are now known, of which nearly 30 seem to have been written before he went to Weimar. Nearly 150 further organ pieces were composed during his nine-year period as court organist, an average of about one every three weeks. Only about 50 others date from the remaining 33 years of his life.

When Bach and his wife moved to Weimar, she was already pregnant. The first of many children, Catharina Dorothea was born in December (*bapt.* 29 December 1708, *d.* 14 January 1774). Her godmother was Johanna Dorothea Bach, the wife of Johann Sebastian's older brother who had looked after him in earlier years in Ohrdruf. (Nearly four years later Bach became godfather – and gave his name – to their son, a second little Johann Sebastian Bach.) Five more of their seven children were also born in Weimar: Wilhelm Friedemann (22 November 1710 – 1 July 1784); twins Maria Sophia and Johann Christoph (*b.* 23 February 1713; the boy died on the day he was born, and the girl died three weeks later, on 15 March 1713); Carl Philipp Emanuel (8 March 1714 – 14 December 1788); and Johann Gottfried Bernhard (11 May 1715 – 27 May 1739).

The household also expanded to take in some students. Just as Johann Sebastian had been taken in by Johann Christoph in Ohrdruf, he now took in Johann Christoph's fifteen-year-old son, Johann Bernhard. Other members of the family that he trained in Weimar include Johann Lorenz Bach, the son of one of his cousins. Bach's brilliant reputation also brought him other organ and harpsichord students. While in Weimar he composed the seven brilliant harpsichord toccatas, BWV 910–916 (unless some of them were written even earlier), and may also have finished writing his first substantial set of harpsichord works in the French style, the six English Suites, BWV 806–811.

Although most of Bach's new colleagues were not composers of lasting value, he was fortunate in having at least one other good organist and composer in town, Johann Gottfried Walther (1684–1748). They were more than colleagues, in fact, since Walther was his cousin (their mothers were both Lämmerhirts). The two men were of almost exactly the same age and their friendship now deepened. Walther was an excellent composer, but was also interested in music as a historical and theoretical subject. He assembled one of the finest musical libraries in Germany. Many years later, in 1732, he published his famous *Musicalisches Lexicon*, the first German-language music dictionary.

Most commentators have assumed it was Walther who played a famous good-natured joke on his cousin. The story is only known from a source dating from 1802, but it had probably been recounted by one of Bach's sons and is likely to be true, especially since it is not entirely to Bach's advantage. Apparently while he was living in Weimar, Bach imprudently – and somewhat impudently – claimed to one of his 'fellow countrymen', who was clearly a musician, that he could play any piece of music at sight. A little trap was therefore set for him. A piece of deliberately unplayable music was composed for the occasion and Bach was invited to breakfast. When he arrived, he found the music lying temptingly near a keyboard and the opening looked deceptively easy. Bach immediately sat down at the instrument and started playing, while his host disappeared into the kitchen to prepare the food – and to listen. Before long, the music suddenly stopped in the middle of a phrase. Bach tried it again, with the same result. 'No!' he cried out, as the friend laughed in the kitchen, 'one cannot play everything at first sight; it is not possible!'[40]

Curiously, at this period Bach seems to have applied for another job, as organist of the Liebfrauenkirche in Halle. The organ was being enlarged to a splendid three-manual instrument with 65 stops. In December 1713 he went there, perhaps on other business, but ended up not only being offered the post, but even accepting it provisionally. However, he did express reservations about how much he would earn (the basic salary offered was about ten per cent lower than his then Weimar salary) and explained that he had not yet asked to be released from his duties at Weimar. After a few weeks of what looks like dilly-dallying, the authorities in Halle firmly told him in February 1714 that they could not increase the salary.[41] On 2 March 1714 the Duke of Weimar offered Bach a musical challenge of a kind he had not yet faced: the responsibilities of being *Conzertmeister* as well as organist. This was followed up by an increase in salary.[42]

It is difficult now to understand exactly what happened. Was Bach playing the two sides off against each other, using the Halle offer to get himself a promotion and salary increase in Weimar? If so, it is the only known case of such manipulation on his part. Or was it rather the duke who, seeing that his brilliant young organist was tempted by the opportunity of moving to a major city and having such a wonderful instrument, the likes of which could never be built in the ducal chapel, shrewdly decided to manipulate Bach instead? That these two events should have occurred in this order suggests that the wily old duke knew his organist well. He could have reasoned that since Bach had been tempted to accept the Halle job for musical reasons, not financial ones, he therefore needed musical reasons to stay in Weimar. And Bach, on his side, may also have been thinking shrewdly. Since this was also the time when he started taking over many of the duties of old *Capellmeister* Drese, perhaps he also saw a good career move opening out before him. The result was that he stayed in Weimar, confident that he had the support of the old duke and that Drese's son would be no threat on the day, surely not far away, when it became necessary to appoint a new *Capellmeister*.

Meanwhile, Walther had been named composition teacher to one of the young dukes in Weimar, also called Johann Ernst like Bach's earlier employer in 1703. But this duke had been born in 1696. By the time Bach arrived in Weimar in 1708, the boy was twelve years old. Not only were his passion for music and his skills as a violinist evident, but he was also showing signs of becoming a talented composer in his own right. From 1711, he studied at the University of Utrecht, in Holland, and was responsible for bringing back to Weimar, when he returned in 1713, many editions printed in Amsterdam of works by Antonio Vivaldi (1678–1741). These included the op. 3 and op. 4 concertos, printed there in 1711 and 1712. While in Amsterdam, he probably also heard the famous blind organist Jan Jacob de Graff, described by Mattheson in 1717 as being famous for playing transcriptions of Italian string concertos on the organ.

Walther later commented that he himself had arranged 78 works by other composers for keyboard, although most are now lost.[43] Over a dozen such concertos survive, based on Italian and German originals by Albinoni, Torelli and Telemann, among others. Appropriately enough, all of them have Italian titles mentioning that they are arranged for the organ ('appropriato all' Organo'), even when there is no pedal part. As for Bach, over twenty keyboard transcriptions of concertos in the Italian style survive, some with pedal part and some without, just like Walther's. Most of his originals were by Vivaldi but there are also works by Benedetto Marcello, Telemann and five works by the young Duke Johann Ernst himself (BWV 592, 595, 982, 984, 987). The duke's compositions had clearly benefited from the lessons he had received in Weimar. The untimely death of this brilliant young man in 1715, at the age of nineteen, was a loss that both Bach and Walther must have felt keenly.

The next year another death occurred, that of *Capellmeister* Drese, on 1 December 1716. Bach reacted swiftly. He was already supposed to produce a new cantata every month, but he now composed three new cantatas in the three weeks before Christmas: *Wachet! betet! betet! wachet!*, BWV 70a, for 6 December 1716; *Ärgre dich, o Seele, nicht*, BWV 186a, for 13 December; and *Herz und Mund und Tat und Leben*, BWV 147a, for 20 December. In these works, Bach was in effect auditioning for Drese's job. However, for reasons that are not clear, the naming of a replacement was postponed. Attempts were made behind Bach's back to get Telemann to come. And then finally, in 1717, Drese's son was named *Capellmeister*. This must have been an exceptionally hard blow for Bach, who in addition to all the organ pieces he had written had composed over twenty cantatas at Weimar. He seems to have decided to leave and to have started looking around for a new post. He now put to good use the excellent relationship he had built up with the reigning duke's young nephew and co-regent, Ernst August of Saxe-Weimar (1688–1748), the son of Bach's first employer in Weimar in 1703, and elder brother of the talented musician Johann Ernst. We have seen that Bach was formally an employee of both Weimar courts, but relations were bad between the two dukes. The irascible Wilhelm Ernst now forbade court employees from working for Ernst August's household, threatening them with heavy fines if they disobeyed.

The previous year, on 24 January 1716, Duke Ernst August had married Princess Eleonore Wilhelmine of Anhalt-Cöthen (1696–1726). Their Weimar residence, the 'Red Castle', was a music-loving household where Bach was a welcome guest. This is probably how he had met the princess's brother, Prince Leopold of Anhalt-Cöthen (1694–1728), who now offered Bach a post. This offer was confirmed on 5 August 1717, with a salary of 400 thalers, nearly double what he earned at Weimar.[44] The arrangement must have been under negotiation for some time before that.

But the duke refused to let Bach go, perhaps because the whole thing seemed like a scheme of his young nephew. Since by law Bach could not resign without his employer's authorization, the result was a stalemate, a stand-off between two proud and obstinate men. The duke considered Bach an insubordinate employee, a schemer, and perhaps disobedient. Bach considered the old duke to have slighted him by appointing Drese's son to the post of *Capellmeister*, and to be now again blocking his career by refusing to release him when he had been offered a better post. The young Prince of Cöthen was not powerful enough to sway the old Duke of Weimar. Only one person could do that: August the Strong, the Elector of Saxony and King of Poland, whose court was in Dresden.

The visit to Dresden

It is unlikely to be a coincidence that Bach managed to go to Dresden a month later. One of the most famous incidents of his life now occurred, his encounter in September (or possibly early October) 1717 with the great French harpsichordist and organist Louis Marchand (1669–1732). This story has often been much distorted.[45]

Marchand, who had been appointed organist to Louis XIV in Versailles in 1708, had been offered an important and well-paid post in Dresden as organist at the court of the king. If Bach was thinking about this organist's post, he must have known that he could not be a favoured candidate. The Dresden ruling family had converted to Catholicism in 1694 in order to strengthen their claim to the Polish crown. The main Dresden court and chapel, the *Hofkapelle*, were therefore Catholic.

The *Conzertmeister,* Jean-Baptiste Volumier (*c.*1670–1728), was in charge of organizing concerts and was a friend of Bach. It was he, apparently, who had written inviting Bach 'with the King's approval'. Volumier had decided to set up a meeting that could only be very politically charged in Dresden, a public musical contest between the French Catholic, Louis Marchand, and the German Lutheran, Johann Sebastian Bach.

Things become clearer when we understand that Volumier was not French himself, but was Flemish (although he had been educated at the French court some 30 years earlier). He was an excellent violinist and had been *Conzertmeister* at the Saxon court in Dresden since 1709. Volumier was not happy with the idea of the Frenchman being appointed, perhaps feeling threatened by the arrival of so eminent a player. Volumier had already taken to calling himself 'Woulmyer' (possibly reviving his Flemish family name, but in any case, an anti-French move). He now spread it about among his German colleagues that 'Marchand spoke sarcastically about all German masters of the keyboard' and hatched a plan 'to humiliate the pride of this Goliath'. But for his plan to succeed, he needed a David, a young player who could be the German champion and be relied upon to win. Bach was clearly the man for this rather dubious task.

As the story is usually told, there was to be an organ contest but Marchand ran away rather than confront Bach. This is flatly contradicted by several sources. It seems that two contests were planned, a first encounter at the harpsichord and another one, the next day, at the organ. It is only the organ contest that never took place.

Bach had apparently written 'a very polite letter' to Marchand inviting him to 'compare their skills at the keyboard'. This last word, *Clavier* in German, refers unequivocally to the harpsichord, not the organ, and another version of the story clearly refers to it as a contest between 'the finest harpsichord masters'. Afterwards, Bach 'took the liberty of inviting Marchand to a friendly contest at the organ, and even gave him a theme which he had noted in pencil on a little piece of paper, to serve as the basis for improvisation, and asked for one in return.' Everyone agrees that this contest never took place. One can only sympathize with Marchand's probable reaction at seeing one of Bach's long, agile, tortuous fugal themes. Discretion being the better part of valour, he left town early the next morning. Bach, although victorious, must have felt a little disappointed, almost cheated, although he entertained the members of the court who had turned up the next day to hear the organ contest, playing to everyone's great satisfaction.

The harpsichord meeting occurred at the house of the prime minister, Count Jacob Heinrich von Flemming (1667–1728):

> With the consent of the king [Bach] was admitted as a listener to the next concert at Court. When, at this concert, Marchand performed among other things a French ditty with many variations, and was much applauded for the art displayed in the variations as well as for his elegant and fiery playing, Bach, who was standing next to him, was urged to try the harpsichord. He accepted the invitation, played a brief preliminary improvisation (with masterly chords) and, before anyone realized what was happening, he repeated the ditty played by Marchand and made a dozen variations on it, with new art and in ways that had not been heard before.[46]

This account goes on by saying that apparently Marchand could not play pieces by Bach. According to J. C. Heck, Bach 'took the Frenchman's composition, placed it upside down, and despite the fact that he had never played it before, played it with the greatest of ease, to the astonishment of everybody present, including Marchand.' This does not ring true and is probably apocryphal. Such a circus trick seems out of character, and it was not Bach's habit to ridicule eminent and genuinely gifted colleagues.

Nevertheless, the rest of the story sounds convincing. Several of Bach's pupils made the point that their teacher always expressed the greatest respect for Marchand and praised his wonderful harpsichord touch. This is what we would expect from a composer who so admired the best French harpsichord playing. Marchand's D minor harpsichord suite is certainly one of the masterpieces of the literature, and Bach not only knew it, he played it to his pupils. One of them (Jakob Adlung) later recalled how enjoyable the occasion was when Bach performed it for him, playing 'in his own style, that is to say very rapidly and ingeniously.'

Bach left Dresden in early October and returned to his blocked situation in Weimar. We do not know whether the post that had supposedly been offered to Marchand (for a salary four times

Bach's current one) really existed. If it did, maybe the king specifically wanted Marchand, or insisted on having a Catholic. Bach might simply have been hoping to be released from Weimar so he could go to Cöthen. Whatever the truth of the matter, he was now frustrated and angry. He insisted that Duke Wilhelm Ernst should release him, wording his demand in rather too blunt terms. Had his visit to Dresden left him with the feeling he had sufficient political support to justify such a perilous way of tackling the problem?

The duke, like Bach's previous employers, seems to have realized that 'since he cannot be made to stay, consent must no doubt be granted for his leaving'. Either way, he thought Bach needed a cooling-off period. On 6 November 1717, he had him arrested and put in prison for four weeks. Then instead of releasing him, the duke threw him out. The court secretary's report is laconic:

> On November 6, the one-time *Conzertmeister* and organist Bach was confined to the County Judge's place of detention, for too stubbornly forcing the issue of his dismissal and finally on December 2 was freed from arrest with notice of his unfavourable discharge.[47]

Bach probably realized that he had won their stand-off and was simply paying the short-term cost, uncomfortable and humiliating, for the long-term victory. He knew that the duke could not keep him in prison for long, and could clearly not reintegrate him into his court functions after such an incident. Moreover, the Prince of Anhalt-Cöthen had already put him on the payroll on 1 August 1717. For Wilhelm Ernst to have kept him there much longer could have created a diplomatic incident. Once again Bach simply had to be patient, and this time he had no choice. But he no doubt meditated on the twists and turns of fortune, whereby one month he could be hailed as the greatest player in Germany, the champion of the national cause at the king's court and the prime minister's house; and the next month be thrown in prison before being dismissed dishonourably.

'VIVAT'

It is easy to assume Bach often drank beer, although perhaps not while he was in prison. As we have seen, Duke Wilhelm Ernst of Weimar had decreed in 1708 that Bach was to receive '30 buckets of beer from our castle brewery' every year as part of his salary. But beer also flows throughout the Bach biography in another way. We have seen that in 1703, when he was appointed organist in Arnstadt, it was specified that part of his yearly salary would be 25 florins 'from the beer taxes'.

Many years later, in Leipzig, the higher school and church officials were also entitled to receive supplementary money derived from a beer tax. Here, for example is the text of a receipt from 1743:

> I have duly received from Mr Christian Friedrich Henrici, regularly appointed Assessment and Liquor Tax Collector of His Royal Majesty in Poland and His Serene Electoral Highness in Saxony, in accordance with the Electoral Saxon Regulation of November 9, 1646, for the period from Low Sunday 1742, to the same 1743, the tax amount for three barrels [of beer] @ 40 groschen, making altogether 5 thalers, that is
> Five Thalers
> in legal tender coins: this I herewith acknowledge and with due thanks give a receipt for the same. Low Sunday, 1743, at Leipzig.
> Joh. Sebast. Bach[1]

There is no indication of what Bach drank in Halle at the fine dinner for the celebrations when the new organ was inaugurated in 1716 (see page 14), but it was probably wine. There are several references to Bach's wine drinking. On 29 September 1721, he became godfather to the son of his colleague, Christian Hahn, Prince Leopold of Anhalt-Cöthen's cellarman.[2] This implies a rather close relationship...

On one occasion in about 1721 he ordered the following bottles:

Rhine Wine . . .
32 measures sold to Mr Capellmeister Bach for 9 thalers

He liked it sufficiently to order a second lot for twice the price, 18 thalers.[3]

We know into what he sometimes poured his wine. Listed among the silverware and other valuables in the inventory of his estate, made after his death, are '6 matching cups, 1 smaller cup, another (chased), and another still smaller, as well as a goblet with cover.' Their combined value, nearly 60 thalers, was considerable; three of the harpsichords, for example, were valued at 50 thalers each.[4]

The Bachhaus in Eisenach has in its collection a remarkable crystal wine goblet, finely engraved with Bach's complex but elegant monogram, involving the initials 'J S B' interwoven with their mirror image (see page 65). There is also the word 'VIVAT'. Since it dates from about 1735 and was made in Dresden, this may have been a present for his 50th birthday, or somehow connected with his nomination as court composer in Dresden at that time.[5]

In 1744 Carl Philipp Emanuel married the daughter of a wine merchant. We can assume that Bach was well received whenever he visited them in Berlin, although there is no trace of their ever having sent him any cases of wine, not even in 1748 to celebrate the birth of their second son, who was named after his grandfather. This young Johann Sebastian Bach (1748–78) became a painter, but died in Rome at an early age; several landscapes by him survive.[6]

On the other hand, Johann Elias Bach (1705–55) did arrange to have wine sent. He was Bach's young cousin. As a theology student at the University of Leipzig he was able to work with Bach from 1737 to 1742. He also became Bach's secretary during these years, and was living in the household. In April 1738 he wrote to his mother about some presents for Johann Sebastian and his wife:

I would very much like to give a bottle of excellent eau de vie to my cousin and some yellow carnations to his wife, who really loves gardening; I know I would thus give them great pleasure...[7]

The following year, on 5 October 1739, he wrote to his sister asking for some wine to send to Bach.

I will repeat my earlier request for the new sweet wine. The good Lord will presumably send you a fine vintage this year, and accordingly I beg you, my dear Sister, most earnestly, to decoct 10 or 12 measures of new sweet wine for me, and send it to me by the express man Herrin, since I would but too gladly give our honoured Cousin this pleasure, having enjoyed many favours in his house for going on two years already.[8]

Being more of a musician than a theologian, as was natural for a Bach, Johann Elias returned to his native town of Schweinfurt in 1743, as cantor of St John's church. Several affectionate yet formal letters survive between him and Bach. The presents of wine seem to have continued. On 2 November 1748, Bach (now aged 63) wrote to thank Johann Elias. The letter has an amusing postscript:

Most noble and most esteemed Cousin,
That you and also your dear wife are still well I am assured by the agreeable note I received from you yesterday accompanying the excellent little cask of expensive new must-wine that you sent me, for which I send you herewith the thanks I owe you. It is, however, greatly to be regretted that the little cask was damaged, either by being shaken up in the wagon or in some other way, for when it was opened for the usual customs inspection here it was almost two-thirds empty, and according to the inspector's report contained no more than six quarts; and it is a pity that even the least drop of this noble gift of God should have been spilled. But, while I heartily congratulate my honoured Cousin on the rich vintage he has garnered, I must acknowledge my inability pro nunc [at this moment] to be in a position to make an appropriate return. But quod differtur non auffertur [deferred is not cancelled], and I hope to have

occasion to acquit my debt in some way. It is indeed to be regretted that the distance between our two cities does not permit us to pay personal visits to each other...

Note: *Although my honoured Cousin kindly offers to oblige with more of the* liqueur, *I must decline his offer on account of the excessive expenses here. For since the carriage charges cost 16 groschen, the delivery man 2 groschen, the customs inspector 2 groschen, the inland duty 5 groschen and 3 pfennig, and the general duty 3 groschen, my honoured Cousin can judge for himself that each quart costs me almost 5 groschen, which for a present is really too expensive.*[9]

No cantata texts refer to beer, but several mention wine. In Ich hatte viel Bekümmernis, *BWV 21, a long Weimar cantata dating from before 1714, the text (which is probably by Salomo Franck) makes use of a pun in German between* Weinen *(weeping) and* Wein *(wine). The whole cantata moves from weeping (beautifully depicted in the opening Sinfonia) to joy. In the tenor aria 'Erfreue dich, Seele' ('Rejoice, my soul'), near the end of the work, the text refers to 'weeping' changing into 'wine' ('Verwandle dich Weinen, in lauteren Wein') and the music flows freely. (An English pun closer in spirit to the original might be 'whining' changing into 'wine'.)*

In Meine Seufzer, meine Tränen, *BWV 13, written over ten years later in Leipzig and first performed on 20 January 1726, the text by G. C. Lehms refers in one of the recitatives to the belief that 'God can quite easily turn the wormwood juice into the wine of joy / And then grant you thousandfold delight.' This text, to be sung by a young boy, is virtuously followed by a solemn and sober aria about groaning and weeping.*

Some of the most amusing references to drinking do not concern alcohol, but occur in Bach's secular cantatas, notably the 'Coffee' Cantata, Schweigt stille, plaudert nicht, *BWV 211. This was written for performance in a coffee shop, in about 1735. The text by the poet Picander presents two main characters: old Herr Schlendrian (a*

bass), and his daughter Liesgen (a soprano) who needs to drink coffee three times a day. 'Coffee! Coffee! Ei! Ei! How good it is! Better than a thousand kisses or muscat wine! Coffee! Coffee! I must have coffee!' Schlendrian replies that unless she gives up coffee, he won't allow her to get married. She admits she would like to find a husband and finally agrees she'll drink no more. But she also secretly promises that all suitors will be rejected unless they come to her and personally promise, and put it into the marriage contract, that she'll be allowed to make coffee as often as she wants. The final chorus suggests that there is no stopping young girls, mothers, and even grandmothers from drinking coffee...

Bach's second daughter, Elisabeth Juliana Friederica, was known in the family as 'Lieschen' or 'Liesgen'. If the 'Coffee' Cantata indeed dates from about 1735, she was only nine. No surviving documents confirm whether she grew up to like coffee, but she did find a husband. On 20 January 1749 she married one of Bach's favourite students, Johann Christoph Altnikol (1720–59). Their first son was called Johann Sebastian.[10]

The first page of Prelude 1 from *The Well-Tempered Clavier*, Book 1, Cöthen, 1722

CHAPTER THREE

Court Composer
and Teacher
(1717–1723)

...the change in my fortunes that took me to Cöthen as
Capellmeister. *There I had a gracious Prince, who both loved and*
knew music, and in his service I intended to spend the rest of my life.
from a letter by Bach, 28 October 1730[1]

Cöthen

Bach's new salary at the court of Anhalt-Cöthen, 400 thalers, was
also supplemented by 'extras'. He was now earning a total of about
450 thalers a year. Since his previous salaries had always been fixed
in florins a note about relative value may be helpful here. Whereas
1 florin contained only 21 groschen, 1 thaler contained 24
groschen. Bach's final Weimar salary had been 250 florins, totalling
5,250 groschen, but in Cöthen he was now earning more than twice
that sum, the equivalent of 10,800 groschen, which was more than
six times what his salary had been ten years before in Arnstadt.
Such an increase no doubt softened the blow to his pride of having
had to spend four weeks in prison, especially since he had already
been on the Cöthen payroll since the beginning of August 1717 and
had thus been well paid during those weeks![2]

His new lodgings were sufficiently substantial that he was able
to earn still further money by renting each week one of the rooms
to the musicians of the court orchestra for their rehearsals, which
he had to direct. He had been released from prison in Weimar on
6 December 1717 and received the first payment for rental of the
rehearsal room for a period starting 10 December.[3] He had lost no
time in moving.

While he was in prison Maria Barbara had been busy preparing the children for the move, packing up the family's belongings, the instruments and Bach's increasingly large collection of manuscripts of his compositions. On 7 August he had received from Prince Leopold a supplementary gift of 50 thalers as a gracious 'recompense' on starting his new job, sometimes referred to as money to help with the moving expenses.[4] The contrast between such generosity and the final indignities at Weimar would have made him feel that he was moving from a place where he was no longer appreciated to one where he was valued at his true worth. He was 32, and several years of professional happiness were about to begin.

The payment for the rehearsal room from 10 December suggests that Bach's hurry to get to Cöthen may have been linked with the prince's birthday, which fell on that day. Did he need to rehearse some festive pieces quickly? Certainly one year later he produced a birthday serenade for the prince, *Der Himmel dacht*, BWV 66a (the music is unfortunately lost), and others were written in the following years.

The task of setting up the new household was largely left to Maria Barbara since Bach immediately went off to Leipzig to examine the organ of the university church, the Paulinerkirche, invited by the rector of Leipzig University. His report, dated 17 December 1717, explains that the instrument had been partly rebuilt and was partly new. Bach's report is typical of many that survive and shows his impartiality as well as his thoroughness.

All the instrument's defects are listed, in particular the uneven voicing of the pipes that 'can and must be corrected immediately' since some pipes spoke much louder than others. The touch of the keyboards was too heavy, and the key-dip too great (so that the keys went down too far when played), although he adds laconically that the keyboards could nevertheless still be played. The instrument was out of tune, but this was to be corrected only 'in better weather than we have been having'. Finally, he reminds the authorities that they should insist on the organ builder guaranteeing his work for one year. Despite these comments, Bach appears basically to be on the side of the organ builder, Johann Scheibe the elder. The various items that had been added but were not in the original plans are all listed, and he insists that the additional sculptures on the organ case, as well as the gilding, have not yet been paid for. A final comment is typical of his eye for practical details: the window behind the organ must now be walled up or covered with a sheet of heavy iron, so as to avoid the organ being damaged by the bad weather.[5]

Back in Cöthen, Bach was able formally to take up his new functions on Christmas Day. He would not have played the organ for the church service since he was not court organist. Prince Leopold's mother was Lutheran but the court chapel was Calvinist, following his father's religion. The services allowed little scope for florid organ playing or elaborate concerted music such as cantatas. Up until this point Bach had been an organist from a family of organists, trained by the greatest organists. He had been kept busy composing organ music, teaching organists, giving organ concerts in other towns, applying for organ posts and, as we have seen, inspecting organs. His life now changed. He had left the profession of church organist behind him for ever. He had, however, now acquired the title of *Capellmeister* that had eluded him in Weimar.

Johann Sebastian and Maria Barbara arrived in Cöthen with their four surviving children: Catharina Dorothea (who was nine), Wilhelm Friedemann (seven), Carl Philipp Emanuel (three) and Johann Gottfried Bernhard (two). The family was soon increased again. Their seventh child, Leopold August Bach, was born on 17 November 1718. The names are a reminder of his two godfathers: Prince Leopold and his 21-year-old younger brother, Prince August Ludwig (1696–1755). The godmother, strengthening the link with the princely family, was their sister Eleonore Wilhelmine, wife of the young Duke Ernst August of Weimar with whom Bach remained on good terms.[6] Unfortunately the baby died ten months later, on 26 September 1719, but his baptism must have been an occasion of great happiness and have encapsulated in a symbolic way the change in fortunes of the Bach family.

Prince Leopold had only recently come of age, on 10 December 1715. He was now 23 and, wishing to make his own mark on his court, relied on Bach to raise the standards of his musical establishment. He had travelled widely and was himself an accomplished amateur musician, playing harpsichord, violin and bass viol, as well as having a pleasing bass voice. He employed nearly twenty instrumental musicians at his court.

Bach was able to put to good use his experience in composing church cantatas, but in a secular direction, by producing cantatas and 'serenadas' to celebrate the prince's birthday and the New Year. He is known to have written at least six such works but they are unfortunately mostly lost.

His duties included the providing of chamber music and at Cöthen he wrote at least ten trio sonatas. Only one is a typical trio with two violins and a bass line for the continuo, the sonata in G major, BWV 1039. Such a trio, despite its name, normally required at least four performers, one to play each of the three musical lines of the trio and a keyboard player to double the bass line and play harmonies (continuo).

Perhaps because there was a shortage of good players, or possibly just because he liked the idea, Bach now adapted the traditional trio sonata to a smaller number of performers, giving the bass line to the left hand of the harpsichord alone, one of the top melody parts to the right hand, and having one other solo instrument to play the third line. Instead of four performers, a trio sonata could thus be played by two. Bach wrote several such keyboard trios at Cöthen, notably the six sonatas for violin and obbligato harpsichord, BWV 1014–1019. These pieces were usually referred to as 'trios for harpsichord with obbligato violin', a clear indication of where he placed the emphasis!

If these works show an increasing concentration, exploiting the musical effects that can be obtained from fewer players than usual, one can imagine what impression was made by the six extraordinary sonatas and partitas for unaccompanied violin, BWV 1001–1006 (dated 1720), and the six perhaps even more original suites for solo cello, BWV 1007–1012. Bach played both instruments. His own violin playing in particular was apparently masterly.[7] But he also liked playing the viola in chamber music for larger ensembles since that way he was right in the middle of the harmony.[8]

In Cöthen, he also wrote pieces for larger ensembles that were probably conceived and intended as chamber music and played with only one player to a part (although they are now often still considered to be 'orchestral' music). The four superb *Ouvertures*, BWV 1066–1069, and three violin concertos, BWV 1041–1043, must have made an impressive effect in the music room of the castle.

Even more striking were the six concertos for differing combinations of instruments that Bach wrote by revising earlier movements and composing some new ones. He compiled a presentation score and dated it 24 March 1721, three days after his 36th birthday. The works were dedicated to the Margrave of Brandenburg who had heard Bach play a couple of years earlier and had asked him to compose some works. The name of Brandenburg has ever since been linked with these wonderful 'six concertos with several instruments', BWV 1046–1051.

Bach travelled with Prince Leopold on several occasions. One of the first such trips was in May 1718, when the prince spent a few weeks in Carlsbad, a Bohemian watering-place. He took along with him not only his *Capellmeister* but also five other musicians and a harpsichord. It must have been something of a working holiday for Bach. Maria Barbara, of course, had to stay at home to look after the children. Two years later, the prince took another such trip, returning home only in July. Bach would have had much news to tell his wife and must have been looking forward to getting home. But when he arrived in Cöthen he was greeted by the news that Maria Barbara had died suddenly. She had already been buried, on 7 July 1720.[9]

They had been married for twelve years and, as far as we can tell, had been a close and happy couple. Having been a Bach herself, Maria Barbara had been a link to his roots. Being the older of the two, she may have been a source of solid support to him, a stabilizing influence on his rather impetuous youthful character. It cannot have been easy living with Johann Sebastian Bach, at any period of his life. His wife had borne the brunt of raising the children, especially when they were young. She had at least six pregnancies in twelve years and had given him seven children, of whom three had died in infancy. With her own distinguished musical ancestry, Maria Barbara Bach should also take part of the credit for the fact that two of their sons, Wilhelm Friedemann and Carl Philipp Emanuel, went on to become – according to their reputations in the eighteenth century – even more eminent musicians than their father. Although history has since readjusted their relative positions, both these sons were musical geniuses of a high order. All in all, Maria Barbara must have been a remarkable woman. She was only 35 when she died.

Catharina Dorothea was eleven and must suddenly have been catapulted out of childhood into the responsibilities of looking after her brothers. Wilhelm Friedemann was nine, Carl Philipp Emanuel, six, and Johann Gottfried Bernhard, five.

When Bach had lost his mother he had been about the same age as Wilhelm Friedemann was now. He had started the keyboard seriously at about this age, when he had to move to Ohrdruf, and Wilhelm Friedemann had also just been given his first lessons. Until this point Bach had perhaps not had much experience of teaching young children, although he had many pupils. He started composing a book of pieces for his son's instruction, possibly because there was nothing more appropriate to hand to use for training a gifted child. The title-page of the 'Little Keyboard Book for Wilhelm Friedemann', one of the most influential volumes in the history of keyboard instruction, is dated 22 January 1720. Its size and format are similar to those of the *Orgel-Büchlein*, which has since acquired an even more special place in the heart of all organ teachers.

A third little pedagogical collection was to follow before Bach left Cöthen, the fifteen two-part inventions and three-part sinfonias, BWV 772–801, dated 1723.

Thoughts about Hamburg

Two months after Maria Barbara's death, the organist at the Jacobikirche in Hamburg died. We do not know when Bach heard about the post, but he no doubt remembered his impression of the town's magnificent organs. The organ in the Jacobikirche was nearly 30 years old, but it was a splendid four-manual instrument with 60 stops and had been well maintained. It still exists.

By November Bach seems to have decided to move to Hamburg if possible. Three years earlier, he had undoubtedly been happy and relieved to have moved to Cöthen, yet it was a small Calvinist court in the middle of nowhere. The chamber music activities had been satisfying, but having done that, he now needed a new challenge. He may also have been thinking about where the children might be sent to school. The educational choices in Cöthen were rather limited. The idea of being in Hamburg, among a community of fine organists and builders, must have tempted Bach more than any other organ post he had yet thought about. The organ had always been his first and greatest musical love.

In November he went to Hamburg and, shrewdly, played a concert in Johann Adam Reincken's church. The authority of the old man (he was 97 years old, but still alert) was immense. Bach may have played the great Fantasia and Fugue in G minor, BWV 542; although doubt has been cast on this idea, it would certainly have been the right sort of work to impress everyone. We do know that he improvised for over half an hour on the theme of the chorale 'An Wasserflussen Babylon', treating the theme in a great variety of ways. Bach did not choose this theme himself, since he was given it as a basis for improvisation, but it offered him an opportunity to pay tribute to Reincken, one of whose finest surviving works is a lengthy fantasia based on the same chorale. Afterwards, Reincken complimented Bach with the words 'I thought that this art [of improvisation] was dead, but I see that it still lives in you.'[10] Everything was therefore looking promising for Bach.

By 21 November his name was on the list of eight official candidates. They were to be formally auditioned on 28 November. Bach was called back to his duties in Cöthen on 23 November, but the Hamburg authorities had no doubt already heard his concert. On the appointed day, three of the other candidates failed to turn up. Since the four remaining players appeared musically unsatisfactory, a message was sent to Bach. Failing to receive a reply from him, the authorities postponed the decision for a week, only to find that he had refused the post.

What happened? The candidate who was finally appointed, Johann Joachim Heitmann, agreed to donate the very large sum of 10,000 marks to the church's coffers. In Mattheson's words he 'was better at preluding with his thalers than with his fingers'. The preacher Erdmann Neumeister solemnly announced from the pulpit that 'even if one of the angels of Bethlehem should come down from heaven, one who played divinely and wished to become organist of St Jacobi, but had no money, he might just as well fly away again.'[11] It appears therefore that Bach had refused to 'buy' the post with a covert bribe, no doubt thinking that rather than his paying to play for them, they should pay for the privilege of hearing him.

Marriage to Anna Magdalena

Returning to Cöthen, Bach soon faced another death in the family. On 22 February 1721, his elder brother, Johann Christoph, died in Orhdruf. Bach was godfather to one of his boys and had trained his eldest son in Weimar. At a similarly difficult time, their father Johann Ambrosius, left with young children, had remarried within less than a year of his wife's death. It was now essential that Bach do so too.

The circumstances under which he met Anna Magdalena Wilcke (1701–60) are unknown. She was the daughter of Johann Caspar Wilcke, a court trumpeter formerly at Zeitz but now at the court of Weissenfels. Here was a point they had in common since Johann Ambrosius Bach had been court trumpeter in Eisenach. Anna Magdalena's elder brother was also a court trumpeter, at Zerbst. Furthermore, there were organists in her family on her mother's side, so she came from musical stock on both sides. She must have arrived in Cöthen in late 1720 or early 1721. The fact that on 25 September 1721 'Johann Sebastian Bach, Capellmeister' and 'Anna Magdalena Wilcke, Singer' are jointly listed as the godparents of the child of Christian Hahn, the Cöthen cellarman, is a sign that they were already betrothed.[12] Their marriage was celebrated in Cöthen on 3 December 1721. She was 20 years old and he was 36.[13]

Anna Magdalena was a professional singer. Bach had possibly come into contact with her in such a musical context. According to his own assessment ten years later, 'my second wife, Anna Magdalena, is a soprano who sings very well'. One unexpected result of the marriage was that the household income increased since Anna Magdalena also received a salary as a court singer. Bach's basic salary was 400 thalers a year, that is 33 thalers and 8 groschen a month. Anna Magdalena's was 26 thalers and 16 groschen, which amounts to 320 thalers a year.[14] She continued receiving her salary in Cöthen until 1 May 1723. We know little else about her, other than the fact that she had a great fondness for gardening (and especially yellow carnations) and was very fond of birds (especially linnets).[15]

On 11 December 1721, eight days after their wedding, Prince Leopold also married. His wife was Friederica Henrietta, the Princess of Anhalt-Bernburg (1702–23). She disliked music and was later referred to by Bach as being an 'amusa'.[16] He found her anything but amusing, nevertheless, since this Latin nickname means 'Muse-less' or 'without a Muse'. His and Anna Magdalena's positions at Cöthen were suddenly looking less interesting and there was now less incentive for him to compose new chamber works. Yet this external circumstance may have simply coincided with his own feelings and ambitions: he had already written a lot of chamber music and had had an opportunity to organize the music-making of the whole castle. He was ready to move on to a greater challenge, such as becoming director of music in a large city.

While he may have entertained such thoughts for his broad career plans, in his own work he now turned in on himself and concentrated on putting his keyboard music in order. He turned his attention to pieces which had not been composed as a result of professional obligations, as had most of his organ works, cantatas (sacred and secular) and chamber music. That Bach thought of his collections in larger groups, no doubt with an eye to possible publication, may already be seen from his having assembled in Weimar a collection of harpsichord toccatas and the English Suites. He now brought together another set of harpsichord suites of somewhat less imposing length and musical complexity, known as the 'little suites' (partly because they did not have lengthy introductory movements, such as those he had provided for the English Suites). These have long been referred to as the French Suites, BWV 812–816, and have always been among the most popular of Bach's works.

More important still, he drew together many of his best preludes and fugues for harpsichord and revised them. Some of these pieces had already figured in a simpler form in earlier manuscripts such as Wilhelm Friedemann's book. Bach imposed on their new versions an order that transcended the value of the individual pieces and assured them everlasting fame. They were incorporated into the most significant volume of keyboard music that Bach – or perhaps anyone else in the history of European music – had ever imagined, the first volume of *The Well-Tempered Clavier*, BWV 846–869, 24 preludes and fugues in all the keys, major and minor. The title-page is dated 1722.

Bach had no doubt taken some fifteen years to write all the pieces in this volume. He completed it by the time he was 37 and it marks the end of an important period of his development (the second volume was ready only about twenty years later). Here for the first time in his harpsichord music we can see the evidence of the organizational power and absolute intellectual grasp which are so apparent in his later works. *The Well-Tempered Clavier* is not merely among the most important monuments in the history of music; it is also one of the most remarkable products of the human mind, taking its place among the finest achievements of western civilization during the eighteenth century.

At the same time, and on a much more modest scale, he started a 'little keyboard book' (*Clavier-Büchlein*) for his new wife. This was the first of what are often referred to as the two 'Little Notebooks' for Anna Magdalena Bach. The first volume took about three years to fill, and the second one was started in 1725. Not surprisingly, these volumes include several songs for soprano, which Anna Magdalena sang to her husband's (or one of her stepsons') accompaniment. The compositions are partly by Bach, but also include works by François Couperin, Georg Böhm and the two Dresden composers Christian Petzold (1677–1733) and Johann Adolf Hasse (1699–1783). Some pieces were copied in by the other members of the family, including Anna Magdalena herself and Bach's two eldest sons. Some of the earliest compositions by Carl Philipp Emanuel are found here.

(It may be helpful at this point to emphasize the difference between the 'Little Notebooks' of Anna Magdalena Bach and *The Little Chronicle of Magdalena Bach*. The two notebooks are collections of music, genuine books from the Bach family that contain compositions written in the handwriting of different family members. They have been published in facsimile and many modern editions. *The Little Chronicle of Magdalena Bach*, on the other hand, is a modern English invention first printed in London in 1925. It was published anonymously and is a charming little book, entirely derived from sources available in the English language at that time. The author was Esther Meynell. This volume was adapted for the famous film by Jean-Marie Straub and Danièle Huillet, *Chronik der Anna-Magdalena Bach*, in 1967. Later English editions contain at the end the phrase 'Those familiar with the known and authenticated facts of Bach's life will realize that certain episodes in this book are imaginary'. Nevertheless, foreign-language editions of the *Chronicle* and much publicity documentation for the film, as well as recent reference books, often still imply that Esther Meynell's *The Little Chronicle* is a document written by Bach's wife.[17])

In 1722, Anna Magdalena and Johann Sebastian were faced with yet another bereavement. On 14 April the last of Bach's three brothers, Johann Jacob, died in Sweden. This was the 'dearly beloved brother' for whom he had written the *Capriccio*, BWV 992, some twenty years earlier. Did he get out the score again? The touching little third movement, marked to be played very slowly indeed (*Adagiosissimo*), 'is a Lamento of his friends'. The musical language of this youthful piece would have seemed simple and unsophisticated to Bach in 1722, but the memories of those difficult days when Johann Jacob and he had gone to the Ohrdruf Lyceum after their parents' death may have once again reminded him of his own children's fate, and of the pressing need to solve the problem of their schooling.

The move to Leipzig

At some point in the summer of 1722 Bach received the news from Leipzig that Johann Kuhnau, the cantor at St Thomas's church and school (the Thomaskirche and the Thomasschule), had died on 5 June. The post carried with it responsibility for the music in four churches. Kuhnau had also been in charge of maintaining the organs of the Thomaskirche and the Nicolaikirche as well as being director of music for the university and for the city. Bach already had contacts with Leipzig and the university, as is shown by the invitation from the rector to examine the organ in December 1717.

Bach was ready for a move for three main reasons: the situation at Cöthen had become less satisfactory; he looked forward to the idea of being director of music in a large town; and his children needed an education. It is easy to imagine him turning over in his mind the advantages and disadvantages of applying for the Leipzig post. The cantor was essentially a teacher; he was expected to teach music, instruct the pupils in catechism and give Latin classes each week. Since Bach could not teach Latin, this last point would have appeared an obstacle.

Bach knew that he could do the musical aspects of Kuhnau's job without a problem. However, the quality of the musicians he would have to work with would, owing to their inexperience and youth, probably be lower than he had had at Weimar or currently had in Cöthen.

On the other hand, in Leipzig his children would be able to receive a free education at an excellent school and have the opportunity to go on to further studies afterwards. Leipzig University, founded in 1409, was one of the most distinguished in Germany. Like many parents who have not had the benefit of a university education, Bach was anxious that his children should have this advantage.

Meanwhile, during August 1722 the Leipzig authorities had approached the famous Georg Philipp Telemann (1681–1767), who had himself been educated at the University of Leipzig and had already been active in the city's musical life. For the last twelve months he had been cantor at the Johanneum in Hamburg and director of music in the city's five principal churches. He was a prolific composer, as is shown by the 1043 cantatas that survive. His formal refusal of the Leipzig offer was received by 22 November and it became clear that another candidate would have to be found. One old city councillor, Abraham Christoph Platz (1658–1728), commented dourly that Telemann was no loss since they needed a teacher not a director of music! Yet Bach may have heard details of this incident. Telemann was a friend of his and Carl Philipp Emanuel's godfather.

The selection process lasted several months, a sign of the difficulties the authorities had in choosing the right man. Four candidates applied early. In order of age, these were:

- Georg Friedrich Kauffmann (1679–1735), the court organist and director of music in Merseburg. Following Telemann's formal refusal, he was invited to perform his official test piece on 29 November.
- Christian Friedrich Rolle, of Magdeburg. He does not seem to have had a university education and was clearly not the strongest candidate, despite being an excellent organist.
- Georg Balthasar Schott (1686–1736), the organist of the Leipzig Neukirche. He had studied at the universities of Jena, from 1709, and Leipzig, from 1714.

- Johann Friedrich Fasch (1688–1758), a former pupil of Kuhnau's at the Thomasschule. He was a friend of Telemann, had studied at Leipzig University and had then been a student of Johann Christoph Graupner (1683–1760). He had recently been appointed *Capellmeister* in Zerbst. He now declared that he would not teach, which seems to have in effect aborted his own candidacy.

The three remaining candidates, Kauffmann, Rolle and Schott, were admitted to the trials, 'especially with regard to teaching'.[18] By January two further candidates had declared themselves, Bach and Fasch's teacher, Johann Christoph Graupner.

One of the members of the Leipzig town council who had to choose the new cantor, Dr Hölzel, expressed the startling opinion that Rolle 'was said to surpass Telemann', but finally declared that he would vote for Graupner. Even Kauffmann, in a nice gesture of fair play, admitted that Graupner was a better man than himself. The authorities agreed, particularly the burgomaster, Dr Gottfried Lange (1672–1748), and the episcopal councillor, Dr Jacob Born (1683–1758). Graupner had been a student at the Thomasschule (from 1696 to 1706) and had thus been a pupil of two former cantors, Schelle and Kuhnau. He had also studied jurisprudence at the University of Leipzig (1704–06). He was a close friend of Telemann and had been *Capellmeister* at Darmstadt since 1712. He also was extraordinarily prolific, as is shown by the 1418 church cantatas that are known, even more than Telemann. He was a perfect second candidate. He successfully performed his two test cantatas on 17 January 1723 and was offered the post. However, Graupner had not yet obtained his release from Darmstadt. The auditions therefore continued.

The stage was set for Bach to present his official test pieces. On the morning of Quinquagesima Sunday, 7 February 1723, he performed two cantatas, *Jesus nahm zu sich die Zwölfe*, BWV 22, and *Du wahrer Gott und Davids Sohn*, BWV 23.[19]

Nevertheless, the Leipzig authorities still hoped Graupner could manage to obtain his release since they really wanted a university-trained teacher. However, in a move reminiscent of what happened to Bach when he wanted to leave Weimar, Ernst Ludwig, Landgrave of Hesse-Darmstadt (himself an amateur composer of some merit), refused to release Graupner (but did not throw him in prison). Instead, in a familiar move, he granted him a significant increase in salary and other benefits. On 23 March 1723, Graupner withdrew his candidacy for the Leipzig post.

Meanwhile, Bach had no doubt returned to Cöthen where, on 4 April 1723, *amusa* died. Although the fact that Prince Leopold's wife had not been fond of music may have had something to do with Bach's decision to leave, her death at this stage cannot have significantly affected his position. He was now too far advanced in the negotiations with Leipzig, and anyway his personal and family reasons for wishing to go to Leipzig were still valid.

On 9 April there were three remaining candidates: Bach, Kauffmann and Schott, none of whom could or would teach Latin. The authorities understood that there would therefore have to be a division of duties. The principle had already been discussed in Telemann's case and had been similarly considered for Graupner. It was therefore accepted for Bach, who was clearly the strongest of the three remaining candidates. Dr Platz wryly commented that 'since the best man can not be obtained, mediocre ones will have to be accepted',[20] a remark that has ever since kept his name alive, poor man. It had been he who had said that Telemann was 'no loss'. Being nearly 30 years older than Bach, and the oldest member of the committee, he was a conservative who hankered after the good old times.

Bach had not yet received his formal release from Cöthen. Prince Leopold granted it willingly but with an expression of personal regret, on 13 April.[21] He also (unlike the Duke of Weimar) let his favourite *Capellmeister* keep his title, since over the next seven years Bach refers to himself on the title-pages of several publications as 'actual *Capellmeister* to His Highness the Prince of Anhalt-Cöthen'.[22]

On 5 May 1723 Bach signed his contract in the council chamber of the old town hall (the present town history museum) and on 8 and 13 May he submitted to some formal interviews (checking his Lutheran orthodoxy, for example).[23] He received the first instalment of his salary on 15 May. The next day, he took up his duties at the Paulinerkirche, the university church where he had approved the organ in December 1717. He now gave there a performance of a cantata, probably *Wer mich liebet, der wird mein Wort halten*, BWV 59. A week later he moved his family and all their furniture from Cöthen to Leipzig.

Anonymous copy, made about 1830, of the well-known portrait of Bach by Elias Gottlob Haussmann. This copy, now in The British Library, was formerly owned by Paul Hirsch and came to The British Museum with his collection in 1946. Two original versions by Haussmann of his portrait survive: one dated 1746 is in the Stadtgeschichtliches Museum, Leipzig, and the other dated 1748 is in the Scheide Collection at Princeton.

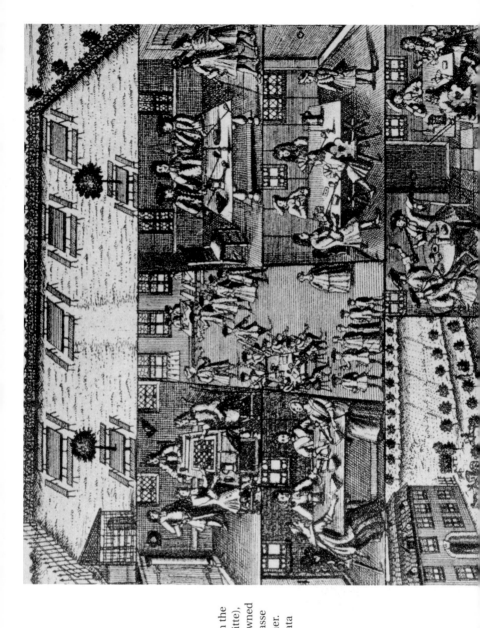

'The Leipzig
Kuchengarten' (in the
suburb of Gaststätte),
drawn in 1746. Owned
by Katherinenstrasse
coffee house owner.
See 'Coffee' Cantata
page 40.

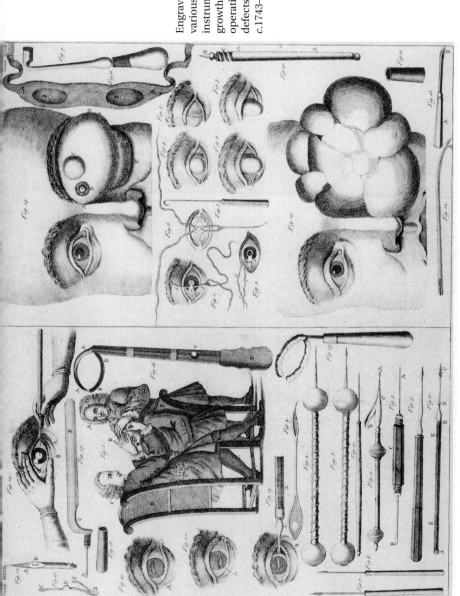

Engraving showing various ophthalmology instruments, eye growths, a cataract operation and other eye defects by R. Parr, c.1743–5.

Autograph of page 19 of the manuscript of *The Art of Fugue*, BWV 1080, Leipzig 1748–9.

'Drum schmauch ich...'

'I smoke my pipe...'. Was Bach a smoker? As a young man of twenty, he is reported as smoking in the street on the occasion of his brawl with the bassoonist Geyersbach, of 'nanny goat' fame. Geyersbach's testimony to the authorities on 14 August 1705 formally says that 'Bach, tobacco pipe in his mouth, was crossing the street'.[1] There is no reason to have mentioned this fact unless it were true.

However, Geyersbach's testimony is contradicted by that of Bach's cousin Barbara Catharina Bach, who was called as a witness on 21 August 1705. The story takes on an extra dimension when we learn that Bach was out walking with her. Not surprisingly, she supports Bach and claims that Geyersbach started the quarrel. 'The witness took Bach by the hand and urged him to leave the scene with her, saying they had something to do together.' Yet, rather curiously, she also raises the quite irrelevant question of the pipe. Bach, she insisted, 'had not a tobacco pipe in his mouth'.[2]

There the anecdote ends. Barbara Catharina seems to have paid particular attention to that pipe. Since she was the elder sister of Maria Barbara, Bach's first wife, the question remains whether Bach was allowed to smoke in the house.

An answer may be inferred from a song written in the 'Second Notebook' for Anna Magdalena Bach: 'Edifying Thoughts of a Tobacco Smoker'. The melody is notated in Anna Magdalena's hand, the bass in Johann Sebastian's. The music is a little minuet in G minor. The text of the curiously sober poem, with six stanzas, discusses the philosophical pleasures of smoking a pipe:

> Whene'er I take my pipe and stuff it
> And smoke to pass the time away,
> My thoughts, as I sit there and puff it,
> Dwell on a picture sad and grey:
> It teaches me that very like
> Am I myself unto my pipe.

Like me, this pipe so fragrant burning
*   Is made of naught but earth and clay;*
To earth I too shall be returning.
*   It falls and, ere I'd think to say,*
It breaks in two before my eyes;
*   In store for me a like fate lies.*

No stain the pipe's hue yet doth darken;
*   It remains white. Thus do I know*
That when to death's call I must hearken
*   My body, too, all pale will grow.*
To black beneath the sod 'twill turn,
*   Likewise the pipe, if oft it burn.*

Or when the pipe is fairly glowing,
*   Behold then, instantaneously,*
The smoke off into thin air going,
*   Till naught but ash is left to see.*
Man's fame likewise away will burn
*   And unto dust his body turn.*

How oft it happens when one's smoking:
*   The stopper's missing from its shelf,*
And one goes with one's finger poking
*   Into the bowl and burns oneself.*
If in the pipe such pain doth dwell,
*   How hot must be the pains of Hell.*

Thus o'er my pipe, in contemplation
*   Of such things, I can constantly*
Indulge in fruitful meditation,
*   And so, puffing contentedly,*
On land, on sea, at home, abroad,
*   I smoke my pipe and worship God.*³

*When Bach visited Halle in 1713, his bill at the Inn of the Golden Ring included 18 groschen for beer and 4 groschen for tobacco.*⁴

There are no references to tobacco in the church cantatas, but Schlendrian, Liesgen's father in the 'Coffee' Cantata, was probably as addicted to his pipe as she was to her coffee.

The inventory of Bach's estate after his death includes four tabatières, *one made of agate set in gold, valued at 40 thalers. No pipes are listed.*[5]

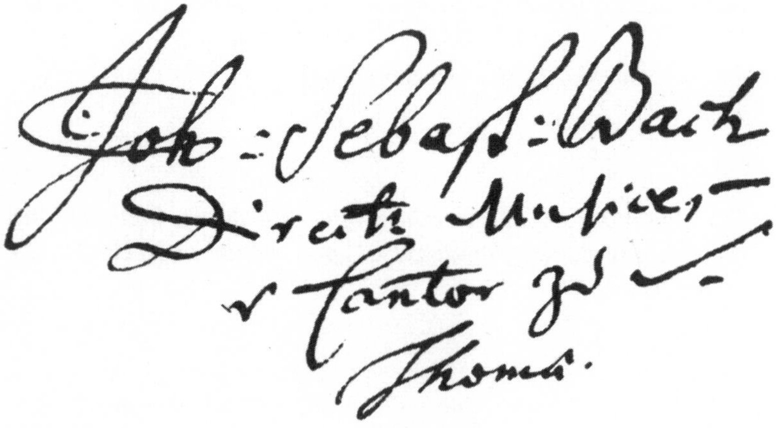
Joh: Sebast: Bach
Director Musices,
u. Cantor zu
Thomä.

Cantor and
Municipal Director of Music
(1723–1750)

And what your pen had writ, the highest art displaying,
Did some with joy and some with envy contemplate.

from a sonnet on Bach by Telemann, January 1751[1]

Leipzig

The Bach family moved to Leipzig on the weekend of 22–3 May 1723. A newspaper report explains that the four carriages of furniture arrived around midday, followed by two further carriages at 2 p.m., bringing Bach and his family.[2] They moved into an apartment on the south side of the Thomasschule. The rector lived on the north side, and the *alumni* (boarding students) up in the attic. The whole building was renovated between 1730 and 1732, adding two extra floors.[3]

The cantor's apartment had a separate entrance on the ground floor, for greater privacy. It was a large house that Carl Philipp Emanuel later described as being 'like a dovecote, and just as full of life'.[4] There was a large reception room and another smaller room. Half way up the staircase were other little rooms. On the first floor were a music room, a living room and a special composing room (the *Komponirstube*). The next two floors also had other smaller living rooms and various bedrooms. The cantor's accommodation included some rooms in the basement, as well as an attic room where the young children probably slept.

The *Komponirstube* was on the south-western corner. It contained a large fixed wall cabinet with four doors and many drawers. This was apparently where Bach kept his manuscripts. It was destroyed in 1903, in an act of astonishing vandalism, because the then officials at St Thomas's wished to enlarge their own quarters. Some highly evocative old photographs survive showing the empty composing room, with its large window looking west.[5] In the process of knocking down the building, four of Wilhelm Friedemann's school exercise books were found (including a book of proverbs and some translations from Greek and from Latin), along with the printed texts of some Bach cantatas dating from 1723 and 1725.[6] One of the few relics that survives today is the heavy wooden door that led through into the cantor's apartment.[7]

On Trinity Sunday, 30 May 1723, Bach performed the cantata *Die Elenden sollen essen*, BWV 75, at the town church, the Nicolaikirche. This first official Leipzig cantata was received 'with much applause' according to another newspaper report.[8] Bach was presented to the whole Thomasschule at 8.30 a.m. on Tuesday 1 June. This was largely a formality since he had already been working with the musicians. Although his private apartment was part of the same building, he was formally welcomed at the main door to the school by the rector and presented to all his colleagues. Then everyone went to the rehearsal room where the students were waiting. The event started with a piece of music performed by the boys and after a lot of lengthy, somewhat sententious speeches (including one in the same vein from Bach) the ceremony closed with another piece.[9]

Bach agreed to pay 50 thalers a year to a certain Carl Friedrich Petzold to teach his Latin classes. Within twelve months this arrangement was found to be unsatisfactory and he was obliged to give Latin dictations himself until a better arrangement could be made. In 1730 this task was finally entrusted to Bach's friend and colleague Abraham Kriegel (1691–1759).

The Thomaskirche could trace its origins back to a monastic foundation dating from 1212 and the school attached to this institution, the Thomasschule, had become a city grammar school in 1543. It included some 50 to 60 *alumni*, and some day pupils. Only the *alumni* normally took part in the music. The post of cantor had existed since the Reformation and its incumbent was third in the school hierarchy. Bach's immediate superiors were therefore the rector, Johann Heinrich Ernesti (1652–1729) and the conrector, Christian Ludovici, who was almost immediately replaced by

Johann Christian Hebenstreit (1686–1756), but all senior officials were ultimately responsible to, and employed by, the town council. Just before moving to Leipzig Bach had had himself made a new seal. His first seal, used on documents of the Weimar period, shows the small letters 'I S B' and a large heraldic design.[10] The first recorded use of the well-known new seal dates from 15 March 1722. He used it throughout his Leipzig years. The large letters 'J S B' are superimposed on their mirror image and the whole has a crown over it.[11] Bach had perhaps admired the seal used by his colleague Rolle on the bottom of the organ report in Halle, in 1716; it interweaves 'J C R' in exactly the same way.[12] A very similar one was used at just the same time by the instrument maker Hermann Tabel, not only as a seal but also as the rose placed in the middle of a harpsichord soundboard (1721). Comparable roses are found in harpsichords built by Jacob Kirckman (1744, 1749) and Johannes Dulcken (1745).[13]

Cantors and their employers

Bach's 27 years in Leipzig, from 1723 until his death in 1750, break down more or less into three periods. His first six or seven years were very active and productive as he established his repertoire of cantata cycles and Passions. The 1730s were more turbulent, marked by conflicts, complaints (by him and about him) and controversies. He seems to have looked around for another job. Partly as relief from the daily grind, he also got more involved in extra-curricular activities, such as directing the university Collegium musicum. During the 1740s a certain resignation set in. He composed much less and became more concerned with a private quest for abstract contrapuntal perfection.

He was not in forward-looking Dresden but in deeply conservative Leipzig, where the town councillors had dismissed Telemann, the most eminent musician in Germany, as being 'no loss', had worried whether Bach's music would be too theatrical, and had recently closed down the opera. Although some of the town council had wanted a teacher more than a director of music, others seem not to have shared this point of view. To their credit it must be said that they had finally agreed to appoint a candidate on his musical merits and then solve the teaching problem. The three principal candidates had all been excellent men and Bach had eventually been elected unanimously by the 28 voting council members. There was evidently a genuine desire to appoint a new cantor who would raise the musical standards, since these were deemed to have fallen during Kuhnau's period of office.

Bach, on his side, is likely never to have forgotten that he had not been the town council's first or even second choice, and that he had been elected only grudgingly. He had the memory of an elephant when he felt he had been slighted. But he was now 38. It may be a sign of his maturity that although the problems he was to face in Leipzig were more extreme and more complex than any he had faced before, he eventually stuck it out.

The previous cantors included eminent men who, unlike Bach, had had intimate links with Leipzig University. Johann Hermann Schein (1586–1630) had been a student there, as had his successor, Tobias Michael (1592–1657), who had also attended the university of Wittenberg, studying theology and philosophy for five years. The next cantor, Sebastian Knüpfer (1633–1676), had not attended university but had unofficially studied philosophy and theology with members of the faculty at Leipzig University and was fully at ease with Latin. In fact, Knüpfer had been regarded as one of the city's leading intellectual figures and was accorded a funeral with full academic honours by the university. His successor, Johann Schelle (1648–1701), had been a pupil at both the Thomasschule and Leipzig University.

Bach's immediate predecessor, Johann Kuhnau (Schelle's cousin), had been exceptionally learned for a musician. He had studied law at Leipzig University and was well versed in Italian, French, Hebrew, Greek and Latin, as well as an excellent self-taught mathematician. Kuhnau was a versatile intellectual of many talents who had also written a witty satirical musical novel. Kuhnau had had conflicts with the town and school authorities as well as with the university. He seems to have been a rather dissatisfied man, complaining constantly and publicly during his last years about the declining musical standards. It was now Bach's task to try and reverse this long-standing situation and raise the standards.

Given this historical context, it is easy to see how some of Leipzig's worthy dignitaries might have been rather condescending towards their new cantor, whose training would have appeared rather light-weight. And it is equally easy to imagine that Bach might have gone into his new post feeling somewhat defensive about his own lack of a university education. At all costs, he was determined that things would be different for his sons.

The two eldest had already started their education at Cöthen's Lutheran Lateinschule. This had not been entirely satisfactory since the better school in Calvinist Cöthen had, naturally, been the Calvinist college. On Monday 14 June 1723 both boys were enrolled at the strictly orthodox Lutheran Thomasschule. The school's archives for 1723 record this important event in their lives: '14 June: Wilhelm Friedemann Bach, born in Weimar, son of Johann Sebastian Bach, cantor of this town, aged 12, enters class three. This same day, Carl Philipp Immanuel Bach, born in the same town, of the same father, enters class five.' 14 For their first Christmas in Leipzig, Bach presented Wilhelm Friedemann with his certificate of enrolment at Leipzig University. The boy was only just thirteen.

Bach later had the satisfaction of seeing four of his sons undertake university studies: Wilhelm Friedemann duly attended Leipzig University from 1729 to 1733, studying mathematics, philosophy and law; Carl Philipp Emanuel studied law there and at the University of Frankfurt, from 1731 to 1734; Johann Gottfried Bernhard became a student at Jena University in 1739; and Johann Christoph Friedrich studied law at Leipzig, from 1749.

Cantata cycles (1723–1727)

In Kuhnau's day, the cantor had been required to produce cantatas each week, performed on alternating Sundays in the Thomaskirche and in the Nicolaikirche. This resulted in each church only having a cantata every two weeks. Kuhnau had also been responsible for organizing another choir, conducted by a prefect from the Thomasschule, that sang motets and chorales at the Matthaeikirche (also known as the Neukirche). Furthermore, the cantor was expected to provide some simple music for the Petrikirche and on important days he could also have to organize music in the Johanniskirche, outside the walls of the city.

Over the years, it had become traditional to provide a cantata every week in both the Thomaskirche and the Nicolaikirche, and Bach thus often had to supervise two cantatas each week, at least one of which was newly composed. As for the Paulinerkirche, it also had its musical traditions but had been the subject of contention for some time.

We have seen that Bach's colleagues in Hamburg and Darmstadt, Telemann and Graupner, were both prolific composers of cantatas, since 1043 and 1418 cantatas survive by each of them, respectively. The reason for this extraordinary output is that in the course of a year the cantata sung on each Sunday and main feast day was supposed to relate to the text of that day's Gospel reading. A complete yearly cycle thus required some 60 cantatas. Composers who were directors of their city's music were sometimes also expected to produce a setting of the Passion story each year, for Holy Week. (Telemann, for example, produced 46 Passions, one for every year from 1722 until his death in 1767.)

Over 200 sacred cantatas by Bach survive (although he often called them 'concertos' or simply '*Musique*', rather than 'cantatas'). There are also two complete Passion settings. Carl Philipp Emanuel later claimed that his father had written five complete yearly cycles for all Sundays and feast days, which implies that over 100 cantatas may now be lost. (He also says his father composed 'five Passion settings'[15] although only two are known; fragments of a third one survive, but the other two are lost.) The chronology of all these pieces was established by Alfred Dürr and published in 1957.[16] This remarkable research showed that during Bach's first four years in Leipzig, from May 1723 until April 1727, he set about his task with extraordinary energy. He also composed additional secular cantatas, works for professors at the university or for the inauguration of the town council, for example, but the vast majority of his output during these years comprises church cantatas for the liturgical year.

Over the twelve months from 30 May 1723 until the end of May 1724 Bach performed at least 50 works, almost all of which were newly composed. (From May to December: BWV 75, 76, 24, 167, 147, 186, 136, 227, 105, 46, 179, 69a, 77, 25, 119, 138, 95, 148, 48, 109, 89, 194, 60, 90, 70, 238, 243a, 40, 64; from January to May 1724: BWV 190, 153, 65, 154, 73, 81, 83, 144, 181, 245, 66, 134, 67, 104, Anh. I 15, 166, 86, 37, 44, 173, 184.) Bach spent his first twelve months deliberately writing a complete cycle for the church year, including a Passion setting. Since in general these works are of a complexity that considerably exceeds the works of Telemann and Graupner, the effort involved is remarkable.

Dürr's research showed that Bach did not write cantatas for the Sundays before Christmas since in Leipzig cantatas were not sung during Advent. Bach had arrived at the Thomaskirche with the scores and performing parts of at least twenty sacred cantatas that he had composed in his last three years in Weimar, several of which were specifically intended for the weeks before Christmas. Rather than have them lie unused, he now revised these works for different feasts.

The three cantatas for the second, third and fourth Sundays in Advent that he had hurriedly composed in December 1716, immediately following Johann Samuel Drese's death, were reallocated, and appeared in reverse order. The third of the Weimar works, *Herz und Mund und Tat und Leben* (originally written for 20 December 1716, fourth Sunday in Advent), was revised in Leipzig for 2 July 1723, the Feast of the Visitation; a cantata for Advent, anticipating the birth of Christ, could easily be recycled for the Visitation, the visit of Elizabeth to the pregnant Virgin Mary. The second, *Ärgre dich, o Seele, nicht* (originally written for 13 December 1716, third Sunday in Advent), appeared in a new form on 11 July 1723. And the first, *Wachet! betet! betet! wachet!* (written for 6 December 1716, second Sunday in Advent), was now revised for 21 November 1723. The Weimar versions of all three works are now lost, but much of the music has been preserved in the Leipzig revisions.

A festive work was of course performed on 25 December, but Bach did not need to write one specially since he already had *Christen, ätzet diesen Tag*, BWV 63, composed in Weimar for Christmas Day. Nevertheless, he did produce two special works in Latin for this important feast: the D major *Sanctus*, BWV 238, and the wonderful setting of the *Magnificat*, BWV 243a. (This is the version in E♭ major, with four extra movements specifically intended for Christmas; the well-known D major version is a revision, dating from five or six years later.)

A two-month gap following 13 February 1724 corresponds to another period when no cantatas were performed in Leipzig: Lent (the weeks before Easter). This pause came to a close in a particularly striking way with the first performance of the St John Passion on 7 April, Good Friday. Here Bach ran into his first major problem with the Leipzig authorities. He assumed this work would be performed at the Thomaskirche and had leaflets printed saying so. He was swiftly contradicted by the authorities and put in his place on 3 April. It was a Leipzig tradition to alternate the church in which the Passion was sung each year and in 1724 it was to be at the Nicolaikirche. Bach protested that there was not enough room (a good practical point) and that the harpsichord there needed repairing, being unusable (a rather weak one since it was easy enough to move an instrument if necessary).[17] One can sense him immediately thinking of the practical implications, but also coming up with anything else he could think of to resist what seemed to him an arbitrary decision.

The authorities insisted on him printing a correction leaflet to announce that the performance would indeed be at the Nicolaikirche.[18] Since funds were immediately released to have the harpsichord repaired, Bach may secretly have felt a certain satisfaction, feeling that the scuffle had produced a small victory for him over civic administration. Although he had lost on the big point, he had won on a small one that would make his life easier in the future, whenever he performed cantatas at the Nicolaikirche.

The council had not finished with him, however. He had omitted to get the text of his leaflet approved and had thus trodden on the dignified toes of Superintendent Salomon Deyling (1677–1755). He was formally reprimanded on 23 May.[19]

Bach continued with the same astonishing energy for his second year in Leipzig, producing another cycle of cantatas. He had now managed to bring the choir of the Thomasschule up to a higher standard. Many of the works in his second cycle contain more lengthy and elaborate choral movements. The period from 1 June 1724 until the end of May 1725 (during which the Advent and Lenten gaps are again evident) saw the composition and first performances of at least 56 works. (From June to December 1724:

BWV 20, 2, 7, 135, 10, 93, 107, 178, 94, 101, 113, 33, 78, 99, 8, 130, 114, 96, 5, 180, 38, 115, 139, 26, 116, 62, 91, 232 (*Sanctus*), 121, 133, 122; from January to May 1725: BWV 41, 123, 124, 3, 111, 92, 125, 126, 127, Anh. I 14, 249a, 1, 249, 6, 42, 85, 103, 108, 87, 128, 183, 74, 68, 175, 176.) In the 24 months since he had arrived in Leipzig Bach had produced half his surviving output of cantatas, composing two complete cycles. On Good Friday (30 March) he had given a second performance of the St John Passion, this time in the Thomaskirche. He had established a substantial repertoire of cantatas that he could draw on in future years.

One interesting work here that it is easy to overlook is the second Sanctus setting in D major, first performed on Christmas Day 1724. Over 30 years later it would be incorporated into the B minor Mass, BWV 232.

The third year in Leipzig shows a noticeable slowing down, with only fourteen new cantatas between 1 June 1725 and 30 May 1726. (From June to December 1725: BWV 168, 205, 137, 164, 79, 57, 151, 28; from January to May 1726: BWV 16, 32, 13, 72, 228, 43.) During this third year Bach may have used some works from his earlier cycles to fill in the apparent gaps but during 1726 he also used eighteen cantatas by his cousin Johann Ludwig Bach (1677–1731), the cantor and *Capellmeister* in Meiningen. Johann Sebastian seems to have taken two years, in fact, to produce his third cycle of cantatas since the works of his fourth twelve-month period in Leipzig, 1726–7, perfectly complement and interlock with the liturgical feasts of the new cantatas for the period 1725–6. (From June to December 1726: BWV 129, 39, 88, 170, 187, 45, 102, 249b, 35, 17, 19, 27, 47, 169, 56, 49, 98, 55, 52, 36a, 20; from January to May 1727: BWV 58, 82, 157, 84, 244.) This third cycle came to a climax with the composition of the St Matthew Passion, first performed on 11 April 1727.[20]

After producing the most monumental of all his works, the St Matthew Passion, Bach's production of cantatas suddenly dropped off. This may simply be because he had now established a large and varied repertory of cantatas for use in future years. It may also be that he slowed down because his interest in the job was waning. A few new works were written during the next two years, but for the twenty years from 1730 until his death in 1750 only about a dozen entirely new cantatas are known. The latest seems to be *Dem Gerechten muss das Licht*, BWV 197, a wedding cantata written some time after 1737. Any cantatas later than this were rearrangements of music written earlier.

In the late 1720s Bach turned his attention towards engraving and printing some of his harpsichord music. The six Partitas, BWV 825–830, his last and greatest set of harpsichord suites, were published at the rate of one a year from November 1726 until 1731, at which point he reissued them as a set. After such immense productivity, it is ironic that the work he now published should carry the indication 'Opus 1' (at that time an opus number was usually reserved for published works, although Bach had in fact already published a cantata in Mühlhausen, in 1708). The first harpsichord partita, dedicated in 1726 to the newly born son of Prince Leopold of Anhalt-Cöthen, carried the title of 'keyboard exercise' (*Clavier Übung*). This was a deliberate homage to Kuhnau who had in his time published two volumes entitled *Neue Clavier-Übung* in Leipzig (in 1689 and 1692), each of which had contained seven partitas. The title had also already been used by Johann Krieger (*Anmuthige Clavier-Übung*, Nuremberg, 1698) and Vincent Lübeck adopted it at about the same time as Bach (1728).

Bach used the same title for later keyboard publications in the same series: the five remaining separate partitas, and the unified volume containing all six, in 1731; the second volume, in 1735, containing the Italian Concerto, BWV 971, and the French *Ouverture*, BWV 831; the third volume, in 1739, containing organ works, BWV 552, 669–689; and a fourth, in 1741–2, containing the 'Goldberg' Variations, BWV 988.[21]

Johann Sebastian was not the only one who had been productive. During their first six years in Leipzig, Anna Magdalena had a child every year, the first six of her thirteen children: Christiana Sophia Henrietta (spring 1723 – 9 June 1726), Gottfried Heinrich (*b.* 26 February 1724, *buried* 12 February 1761), Christian Gottlieb (*bapt.* 14 April 1725, *d.* 21 September 1728), Elisabeth Juliana Friederica (*bapt.* 5 April 1726, *d.* 24 August 1781), Ernestus Andreas (*bapt.* 30 October 1727, *d.* 1 November 1727) and Regina Johanna (*bapt.* 10 October 1728, *d.* 25 April 1733). Only two of these were to live past the age of five: Gottfried Heinrich, who showed clear musical talents when young and played the harpsichord well but was 'feeble-minded', and Elisabeth Juliana Friederica ('Liesgen'), who later married Bach's pupil Altnikol and eventually took care of Gottfried Heinrich after Johann Sebastian's death.

When he gave the first performance of the St Matthew Passion, Bach had just turned 42. Over the previous twenty years, he had composed a vast amount of music – some 200 organ pieces, the seven harpsichord toccatas, the six English Suites, the six French Suites as well as other smaller suites, the first volume of *The Well-Tempered Clavier*, the six sonatas and partitas for solo violin, the six suites for solo cello, the four orchestral *Ouvertures*, the six Brandenburg Concertos, well over 100 cantatas, the St John Passion and the St Matthew Passion, as well as a host of other works. He had reached a watershed in his life and things were never quite the same afterwards. Whatever the causes, there are signs that he felt somewhat artistically exhausted and had reached a sort of mid-life crisis. Perhaps this was sparked off by the death of his sister Maria Salome in 1727 – she had been the last of his seven brothers and sisters still alive.

First difficulties in Leipzig (1723–1733)

Kuhnau had had the right to play for various university services and for this had been paid 12 florins as a supplement to his income. During the year between his death and Bach's appointment, the young organist Johann Gottlieb Görner (1697–1778) had taken over these tasks and been granted the title of director of music at the university church. Bach saw this as an infringement of his own rights and he was not a man to take such things lightly. He had therefore laid claim in 1725 to what he saw as the traditional rights of the cantor, starting with the 12 florins a year for the two years he had already been in Leipzig. This might at first sight seem small-minded of him. His concern becomes clearer when we learn that as cantor, strictly speaking, he received only 87 thalers and 12 groschen salary, whereas in Cöthen he had earned up to 450 thalers. In Leipzig he also had the usual allowances in kind – this time including wood, corn, wine and candles – and he was entitled to receive 5 florins a year from a trust fund left in 1612 by a rich widow, Sabine Nathan. His full earnings each year depended on many extra payments, known as *accidentia*.

According to one of his own letters, dated 28 October 1730, his income in Leipzig normally came to about 700 thalers a year.[22] Although he could thus earn a considerably better living than in Cöthen, it must be remembered that Johann Sebastian and Anna Magdalena had there jointly been earning about 770 thalers a year. This sheds a different light on Bach's financial concerns and explains his attitude towards the *accidentia*.

Bach's problems with Görner had started in his first year. On 14 September 1725, hoping to solve the problem, he had written directly to August the Strong in Dresden. He was no doubt taking advantage of the fact that a few days later, on 19 and 20 September 1725, he would be in Dresden to play some prestigious organ concerts. But by addressing the king he had overreached himself. Subsequent reports brought to light the fact that he had not been fulfilling to the letter the cantor's supposed duties in the university church, or at least not in the way Kuhnau had done; he was refusing to accompany the prayers in person, for example, sending a deputy instead. When the royal decision arrived on 21 January 1726 he learned that he had lost.

In October 1727, the university commissioned a funeral ode for Princess Christiane Eberhardine. The result was *Lass Fürstin, lass noch einen Strahl*, BWV 198 (described at the time as being 'in the Italian style').[23] Bach played the harpsichord himself at the performance. Unfortunately, this commission opened once again the conflict with Görner, who on 9 October objected to Bach's participation, claiming that it would cause both his reputation and his income to suffer. Since the ceremony was due to take place on 17 October, Görner must have realized he would not be able himself to compose the necessary music so rapidly. He therefore simply asked to be paid half of Bach's fee as a compensation. Bach of course refused but a compromise was reached. They seem to have patched things up since in 1729 the selection committee that chose Görner as organist at the Thomaskirche included the cantor.

Bach also had a say, again in 1729, in naming Görner's replacement as organist at the Nicolaikirche. In a seemingly unimportant little incident resulting from this game of musical chairs, he voted against the young and inexperienced Johann Adolph Scheibe

(1708–76), the son of the organ builder Johann Scheibe the elder, whose instrument for the university church Bach had examined twelve years earlier. As we shall see, young Scheibe got his own back eight years later, in 1737, publishing the most extended criticism of Bach's musical style that appeared in his lifetime and sparking off a lengthy controversy.

Despite all his efforts to fulfil his duties honourably, Bach could not avoid upsetting people. One particular bone of contention was the subject matter (along with the musical thematic material) to be used in the cantatas. On 8 September 1728 he was formally reprimanded and reminded that once the preachers had chosen a theme and a chorale for the upcoming cantata, he should conform to their decision. Bach's reply, dated 20 September, is entirely worthy of him. He recalls that his predecessors had had free choice in such matters, as long as they had taken into account the Gospel reading for the day. The best defence being an attack, he then accuses the subdeacon of the Nicolaikirche, Gottlieb Gaudlitz (1694–1745), of 'innovation', a useful counter-charge in conservative Leipzig.[24] He seems to have patched up his differences with the subdeacon, as he did with Görner, since Gaudlitz later baptized two of his children, in 1732 and 1737. Bach may have been highly sensitive when his rights were infringed, but he was also a pragmatist.

Two months later, on 23 November 1728, Prince Leopold of Anhalt-Cöthen died. Bach's funeral music for his old patron and friend (*Klagt, Kinder, klagt es aller Welt*, BWV 244a) was performed only four months later, on 24 March 1729. Written for double chorus, this work was apparently particularly moving. It is now lost but much of it had been drawn from the choruses of the St Matthew Passion, with other movements taken from the previous funeral ode he had written, less than two years earlier, for Princess Christiane Eberhardine. With Prince Leopold's death, Bach's title of *Capellmeister* to the court of Anhalt-Cöthen lapsed (he last used it in 1730 on the title-page of the fifth Partita), but shortly afterwards he was given the honorary title of *Capellmeister* to the court of the music-loving Prince Christian of Saxe-Weissenfels (1682–1736).

The situation at the Thomasschule had become uneasy during 1729 and was brought to a head by the death of the rector, Johann Heinrich Ernesti, on 16 October. Bach hurriedly wrote the double-choir motet *Der Geist hilft unser Schwachheit auf,* BWV 226, for his funeral on 24 October. Thereafter, the situation went from bad to worse and within a year he had reached breaking point.

He had been neglecting his duties and was formally accused on 2 August 1730. The person who taught Latin for him was incompetent; he had sent a choir of students away 'to the country'; he had himself gone away without asking permission. Councillor Steger, who at the time of Bach's appointment appears to have been one of his allies, bluntly summed up the situation: he declared that 'the cantor does nothing, refuses to offer any explanation and doesn't give singing lessons, that various accusations are accumulating and changes are necessary, once and for all.' Councillors Born and Hölzel agreed. It was proposed to reduce Bach's already small salary. This was carried unanimously, with one councillor adding that Bach was 'incorrigible'.[25]

Bach spent three weeks preparing his reply, the longest and most detailed musical document from him that survives. This is the famous 'Short but most necessary draft for a well-appointed Church *Music*, with certain reflections on the decline of the same' (23 August 1730).[26] It is fierce, logical, angry and precise. His sense of sarcasm comes to the fore as he explains what musical forces he ideally needs for performing the weekly cantatas, and what he can actually call on in practice. The difference between the two is startling. In the past (here he refers specifically to his predecessors Schelle and Kuhnau) the deficiencies had been made up by paying to bring in outside instrumentalists such as university students. Such payments were no longer authorized and yet he was expected to produce more elaborate and complex music, in more modern styles. The situation was impossible. Who, he asks rhetorically, would perform a service for nothing? To see how things should be done properly, 'one need only go to Dresden'.

The document reaches a climax when he describes the students at the Thomasschule who are supposed to perform each Sunday, providing music for four churches in Leipzig. Out of 55, only seventeen 'can be used' for music-making, twenty 'cannot yet be used' since they first need further instruction, and seventeen 'are not musicians at all' and are 'incapable' (one boy appears to have been forgotten since this makes only 54). These boys are all meticulously listed by name. The fact that some of them have the same names as members of the town council indicates another, unsuspected layer to the problem. Fortunately, the burgomaster's son, Lange, is among the seventeen who 'can be used'; the sons of some of the other worthies (for example, Hebenstreit, the son of the conrector) are 'incapable'.

The bluntness of Bach's reply to the accusations shows that he felt they were unjust. Two months later, on 28 October 1730, he wrote to his old friend Georg Erdmann asking for help.

> I note that (1) my job is not as well paid as I had been told, (2) that many of the *accidentia* that should come with the job do not do so, (3) the cost of living is very expensive, and (4) that the town authorities are given to whims and have little taste for music. I must live in virtual perpetual conflict, the object of envy and persecution. I will therefore be obliged to seek my fortune else-where.[27]

He also adds the now famous complaint that when the weather is good not enough people die, causing his income to fall by as much as 100 thalers! The remark is startling, but underlines his essential reliance on the *accidentia*, such as well-paid music for funerals and weddings, to earn a decent living. He ends by noting somewhat nostalgically that he could live in Thuringia just as well for only 400 thalers, since life in Leipzig is so expensive.

However, shortly after this a new rector was named at the Thomasschule, Johann Matthias Gesner (1691–1761). This was good news since they had known each other in Weimar. Gesner was one of Bach's great admirers.

An increasing number of Bach's students were now seeking jobs and asking him for testimonials. Twenty-six such recommendations survive, but he must have written many more, conscientiously trying to help the young musicians he had trained, whatever their talents. The language chosen for these little texts is measured and far from automatic. Like the wording of his numerous reports on new organs, his judgement is always courteous but scrupulously honest. The real musicians, such as Johann Ludwig Krebs or Johann Christoph Altnikol, get testimonials that are full of warm praise and detailed enthusiasm, where Bach's affection is evident. Some are less enthusiastic and tinged with irony, such as the recommendation for the less-talented Johann Christoph Dorn, dated 11 May 1731:

> The bearer, *Mons.* Johann Christoph Dorn, student of Music, has asked me to give him an *attestatum* concerning his knowledge in *Musicis.* I have found after testing him that he has a reasonably good command of the Clavier and of other Instruments, and is therefore in a position to offer service to God and the *Republic*, so I must not refuse his request, but must instead testify that with his good natural talent he promises to become, some years from now, a competent Musician.[28]

If many of his pupils were of this sort, it is easy to understand why Bach was losing interest in his work at the Thomasschule, and was feeling frustrated by the lack of good young musicians with whom to work.

In 1729, two years before writing this recommendation for Dorn, he had taken over the musical direction of the old Collegium musicum. (The first known performance under his direction was on 12 June 1729.) The Collegium had been founded by Telemann in his student days, nearly 30 years earlier. Working with this group brought Bach into contact with young instrumentalists of a far higher standard than the average boys of the Thomasschule. Several of his best ex-students joined the Collegium to continue working with him, now that they were enrolled at the university. Among them was the nineteen-year-old Wilhelm Friedemann. Drawing on the skills of his sons and his finest pupils at this time, Bach produced the brilliant concertos for one, two, three and four harpsichords. It is easy to imagine his delight in working with his son's friends, especially since Wilhelm Friedemann must have shone as the most brilliant player among them.

The Collegium concerts took place once a week on Friday evenings from 8 to 10 o'clock, in the gardens of Gottfried Zimmermann's coffee house. (This was destroyed by allied bombing during the Second World War.) On special occasions, a second concert was also held on the Tuesday evening. Here he also performed much chamber music and certainly gave the first performance of one of his most humourous works, the 'Coffee' Cantata, BWV 211. Bach's title was 'Schlendrian and his daughter Liesgen, a comical cantata'. The opening words, 'Schweigt stille, plaudert nicht' ('Be silent! Stop talking!') were no doubt addressed to the chattering audience in the noisy coffee house. Bach continued directing the Collegium, with interruptions, until Zimmermann died (on 30 May 1741).

Thoughts of Dresden (1731–1736)

The tensions at the Thomasschule had quietened down but the essential problems remained. Bach's long complaint to the Leipzig town council in 1730 had contained the telling phrase 'one need only go to Dresden'. In September 1731, he played organ concerts again in Dresden. When the old prince-elector, August the Strong, died on 1 February 1733, he was succeeded by his son Frederick August II (1696–1763). Moreover, Bach's friend Christian Petzold also died at the end of May. He had been organist of the Sophienkirche in Dresden, where the organ was a splendid new instrument on which Bach had played his concerts in 1725 and 1731.

As he had so often in the past when a good organ job was available, he jumped at the opportunity. But times had changed. The official letters that now went off to Dresden from the Bach household were not signed by him but by the 23-year-old Wilhelm Friedemann. He had finished his university studies and needed a job. Wilhelm Friedemann was named to the post at the end of June 1732.

In about 1733 Bach was painted with three of his sons, if we can trust the recent identification of an undated group portrait, painted by Bach's exact contemporary, the Dresden painter Balthasar Denner (1685–1749). Four musicians are shown, a middle-aged man and three boys. Johann Sebastian, if it is he, is seated on the left, holding a cello. The three boys are standing and shown in order of increasing size, from left to right. They hold a violin, a flute and a violin, respectively. Judging from their apparent ages these could be, in order, Bach's fourth, third and second sons, Gottfried Heinrich (8–9 years), Johann Gottfried Bernhard (17–18) and Carl Philipp Emanuel (18–19). This hypothesis would explain Wilhelm Friedemann's absence by his having moved to Dresden.

Bach may have sensed the irony of his not applying for the organ post in Dresden yet he had his own sights set on a higher prize. The official mourning period for the old prince-elector was from 15 February to 2 July 1733. During these months Bach composed an important new work. On 27 July 1733, he wrote directly to the new young prince-elector and sent him a particularly splendid setting of the Kyrie and the Gloria. These two movements (which would later become the two opening parts of the B minor Mass, BWV 232) were highly appropriate since the Dresden court was Catholic, yet they were also the traditional two Latin movements from the Ordinary of the mass that were not out of place in a Lutheran service. It was a politically astute attempt to curry favour, in the hope of obtaining a court appointment in the city where his son had just been named organist.

These two pieces that form the Lutheran *Missa* contain a great variety of styles. Bach was showing what he could do. The first movement ('Kyrie eleison'), for example, is a modern fugal concerto movement, whereas the third movement, to the same text, is in the severest of old-style counterpoint. Between the two, the setting of 'Christe eleison' is written in the most up-to-date Italianate operatic style.

Some of the more virtuoso arias, such as the 'Laudamus te', may have been specifically written for the principal soprano of the royal chapel, the great Venetian singer Faustina Bordoni (1700–81). She had recently married the Dresden *Capellmeister*, Johann Adolf Hasse. The extensive violin solo in the 'Laudamus te' would have been specially conceived for Johann Georg Pisendel (1687–1755), whom Bach had known since at least 1709. The flute solo in the 'Domine Deus rex caelestis' would have been played by Pierre-Gabriel Buffardin, the flute teacher of Bach's brother Johann Jacob in Constantinople, whom Bach had probably known since at least 1717. It seems likely that Wilhelm Friedemann arranged for a performance of this *Missa* in Dresden about this time. The orchestral parts contain pages in the handwriting of Johann Sebastian, Anna Magdalena, Wilhelm Friedemann and Carl Philipp Emanuel.

Bach's dedicatory letter begs the new prince-elector not to judge the music according to its 'poor *Composition*'.[29] He recalls that in

Leipzig he has had to suffer various unmerited affronts. This text is more than usually obsequious, even by the standards of the time, but this does not stop Bach from bluntly asking to be named a member of the royal chapel.

When no appointment in Dresden seemed to be forthcoming, Bach kept up – rather laboriously – with a series of courtly works in Leipzig, notably the following eight secular cantatas in honour of the prince-elector or his family, all performed by the Collegium at Zimmermann's:

- 3 August 1733: *Frohes Volk, vergnügte Sachsen*, BWV Anh. I 12 (the music is lost), written for the prince's birthday.
- 5 September 1733: *Hercules auf dem Scheidewege*, BWV 213, a *drama per musica* for the eleventh birthday of the prince's son, Friedrich Christian (1722–63).
- 8 December 1733: *Tönet, ihr Pauken!*, BWV 214, a *drama per musica* for the birthday of the Electress Maria Josepha, the prince's wife.
- 19 February 1734: *Blast Lärmen, ihr Feinde*, BWV 205a (the music is lost), a *drama per musica* to celebrate the coronation of the prince as King of Poland.
- 24 August 1734: an unknown work was performed in the new king's honour.
- 5 October 1734: *Preise dein Glücke*, BWV 215, an *Abend-Music*, again written in the new king's honour. It was performed by the students of the Collegium in the presence of the king, his wife, and their son. The concert started at 9 o'clock at night. It was described by one witness as an 'evening serenade with trumpets and drums'.[30] On this occasion, the Leipzig city trumpeters were called in as reinforcements.
- 3 August 1735: *Auf, schmetternde Töne*, BWV 207a, for the king's name day.
- In October 1736: *Schleicht, spielende Wellen*, BWV 206, for the king's birthday.

This effort was all to no avail in terms of a new job in Dresden although for his trouble Bach was eventually, on 19 November 1736, awarded the honorary title of court composer in the royal chapel, with no salary attached.

Twelve days later, on 1 December 1736, Bach went to Dresden to inaugurate a new organ by the great builder Gottfried Silbermann (1683–1753), in the Frauenkirche. The concert took place from 2 to 4 o'clock in the afternoon. Bach's formal letter of appointment to the title of court composer was transmitted to him by Baron (later Count) Hermann von Keyserlingk (1696–1764), the Russian Ambassador. Keyserlingk clearly had some close contact with the Bach family since two years later Carl Philipp Emanuel was offered the opportunity to accompany a 'young gentleman', Keyserlingk's son Heinrich Christian, on a foreign trip.

Ever practical, Bach recycled much of the music of the secular cantatas he had recently performed at Zimmermann's into the splendid series of six sacred cantatas now known as the Christmas Oratorio, BWV 248. In their new guise, they were first performed on 25, 26 and 27 December 1734 and 1, 2 and 6 January 1735. Bach the cantor was quite happy to praise God using secular music written in honour of a prince and performed in a coffee house, or to cele-brate the birth of Christ using works written for the birthday of the prince's wife.

Between 1730 and 1736, Johann Sebastian and Anna Magdalena had another five children, three of whom died young: Christiana Benedicta Louisa (*bapt.* 1 January 1730, *d.* 4 January 1730), Christiana Dorothea (*bapt.* 18 March 1731, *d.* 31 August 1732), Johann Christoph Friedrich (21 June 1732 – 26 January 1795), Johann August Abraham (*bapt.* 5 November 1733, *d.* 6 November 1733), Johann Christian (5 September 1735 – 1 January 1782). These were also the years during which the talent of young Gottfried Heinrich was becoming evident although there were not yet signs of his later mental problems.

Johann Gottfried Bernhard was now twenty. In May 1735, his father's recommendation was instrumental in getting him named to the post of town organist in Mühlhausen, where Bach had briefly been organist at the church of St Blasius, nearly 30 years before. The organ at the Marienkirche had just been rebuilt, and Bach trav-elled there to inspect it in June 1735.

In 1735 Bach reached the age of 50. At the end of the year he put in order the famous 'Bach family archives', with its list of over 50 musicians with the name Bach.[31] His own position is number 24 on the list. Among the latest entries he proudly listed his six living sons with their dates of birth:

- No. 45. *Wilhelm Friedemann Bach*, eldest son of Joh. Seb. Bach (no. 24), is at present Organist of the Sophien Kirche in Dresden. Born 1710, 22nd Nov.
- No. 46. *Carl Philipp Emanuel Bach*, 2nd son of Joh. Seb. Bach (no. 24). Lives in Frankfurt-on-the-Oder, as a *Studiosus* and teacher of the *Clavier*. Born 14 March 1714. [This is an error; he was born on 8 March.]
- No. 47. *Joh. Gottfried Bernhard Bach*, 3rd son of Joh. Seb. Bach (no. 24), is Organist in Mühlhausen at the Marien or Upper Church. Born 11 May 1715.
- No. 48. *Gottfried Heinrich Bach*, 4th son of Joh. Seb. Bach (no. 24). Was born 26 Feb. 1724. Similarly *inclined* toward music, especially Clavier-playing.
- No. 49. *Joh. Christoph Friedrich Bach*, 5th son of Joh. Seb. Bach (no. 24). Born 21 June 1732.
- No. 50. *Joh. Christian Bach*, 6th son of Joh. Seb. Bach (no. 24). Born 1735, 5th Sept.

It is touching to see him include the last two, so sure was he (and rightly) that they would become musicians. Johann Christian was only a few months old. One can also see that, even though the mother of the first three was also a Bach, these boys appear to have only a father...

Johann Gottfried Bernhard did not remain organist in Mühlhausen for much longer than Bach himself had been since, less than two years later (and again thanks to his father's support), he became organist at the Jacobikirche in Sangerhausen. This was the very post that Johann Sebastian had so nearly obtained at the start of his career, in 1703. In his recommendation letter, Bach even goes as far as to ask 'Who knows whether a Divine Decree is not at work here...perhaps Divine Providence is taking a hand',[32] a nice touch of gentle manipulation of his son's future employers!

In late 1735 and early 1736 Bach revised the St Matthew Passion. On Good Friday of 1736 it was given in the form we know today. His life at this time was largely taken up with the weekly round of repeat performances on Sundays of sacred cantatas he had written in earlier years. He also did a considerable amount of private teaching. It is estimated that he had about 80 private students during his years in Leipzig.

Just before Easter 1736, he published a series of sacred songs in a volume prepared by a former student of the Thomasschule, Georg Christian Schemelli (1676–1762). The music for 69 songs is given, for which Bach certainly at least prepared the figured basses and revised some of the melodies. A few of the pieces, including the famous songs 'Dir, dir Jehovah', BWV 452, and 'Komm, süsser Tod', BWV 478, are entirely his own compositions. The other songs are among the least known part of Bach's output, but they are beautifully crafted.

Trouble with the rector (1736–1738)

Unfortunately for Bach, his friend Johann Matthias Gesner, the rector who had succeeded Johann Heinrich Ernesti, had left in 1734 to teach at the newly founded University of Göttingen. The young deputy rector, Johann August Ernesti (1707–81), was promoted to rector. It is confusing that he had the same name as the earlier rector, but they do not appear to have been related.

The new Rector Ernesti was a man of outstanding intellect and a fine scholar. This did not stop a violent quarrel breaking out with the cantor in 1736. It was to be the bitterest episode in Bach's whole career. Ernesti, to his credit, was trying to raise the academic standards of the school, just as Bach had been trying to raise the musical standards. But Ernesti thought that music distracted the boys from more serious studies. Moreover, the row was a conflict of generations. At 51, Bach was facing an ambitious young rector of 29.

The argument concerned two boys who, to add to the confusion, were both called Krause. The head prefect, Gottfried Theodor Krause (who six years earlier had figured on Bach's 1730 list of the seventeen most competent pupils), had been involved in an infringement of discipline, had been sanctioned, and then seems to have run away. Ernesti seized the initiative and replaced him by a boy called Johann Gottlieb Krause. This latter Krause, according to Bach, was musically 'incompetent'. In May 1729, Bach had given his initial judgement on this boy when he entered the school: 'Johann Gottlieb Krause, of Grossdeuben, aged fourteen years, whose voice is somewhat weak and proficiency indifferent.'[33]

The superficial details of the dispute with the rector now appear rather sordid. Hidden behind them is the fact that the school's new regulations, on which Johann August Ernesti relied for his authority in the matter, dated from 1723 (revised in 1733), whereas Bach had never accepted them since they had a detrimental effect on his status and his earnings. Indeed, the then rector, Johann Heinrich Ernesti, had also opposed the new ones and they had never been formally ratified. In Bach's view, this made the new rules invalid. He preferred to refer to the old regulations, dating from 1634.

Bach's vigorous defence of the cantor's traditional right to name the senior prefect, who had to help him in the rehearsals and conduct the choir in his absence, was thus more than a mere tempest in an academic teacup. The new Rector Ernesti had failed either to consult the cantor or to inform him of his decision to appoint the 'incompetent' Krause. This was the spark that ignited Bach's explosive reaction, but the real dynamite of the situation was the more fundamental matter of the new regulations, a problem that had been nagging for thirteen years.

The pressure built up during June and July 1736, finally exploding on 11 August during a performance in the Nicolaikirche, thereby creating a public scandal. The rector and the cantor rapidly entrenched themselves in extreme positions and became implacable enemies. On the one hand, Ernesti developed a hatred for everything and everyone connected with music, insulting the pupils who practised their instruments as well as threatening the boys with public whipping and humiliation, even expulsion from the school, if they sang for any other prefect except Krause. On the other hand, Bach apparently said he would not change his position, 'no matter what the cost',[34] developed a profound dislike for the many students who were uninterested in music and began deliberately neglecting all his non-musical duties.

The three complaints that Bach made to the town council, dated 12, 13 and 15 August,[35] explicitly state that he felt he had been publicly humiliated since the pupils of the school, fearing the rector, refused to sing at a service despite his explicit instructions. This was intolerable. If we can believe his comments, the 'incompetent' Krause whom Ernesti had imposed as prefect was a profligate good-for-nothing who had built up substantial debts and, what was worse, could not even beat time correctly. Subsequent events suggest Bach was employing tactical exaggeration here. However he also unwisely went a step further in his comments, hitting below the belt. He suggested, and put in writing, using not too subtle innuendo, that the rector had always had a 'particular liking for Krause' ('Da nun der Herr Rektor vor ihme, Krausen, iederzeit besondere Geneigtheit spühren laßen').[36]

Ernesti, stung by all these accusations, sent a very lengthy reply two days later, and another on 13 September. He did not reply at all to the underlying innuendo, preferring to rely for his best defence on as powerful a counter-attack against the cantor as he could muster. He says first that Bach has on previous occasions 'out of personal prejudice, skipped over promoting a student of real merit'. He claims that the cantor already has no real authority over the boys and that if Krause made a mistake in beating time it is certainly because 'Mr Bach had the intention and desire that he should make one'. In between his honeyed phrases to the town council Ernesti describes Bach as a devious, stubborn, tendentious, unreliable and rather hysterical man, as someone who does not keep his word and is vindictive to students he doesn't like. The cantor's character is called into question. Moreover, Ernesti bluntly accuses Bach of lying: 'How easily one betrays oneself in a lie!'[37]

Bach was never more formidable than when he was really angry. He became logical, cold and inexorable, not allowing a single point to be overlooked. Unfortunately, Ernesti was the same sort of man. He was not inclined to give in, preferring to write another rebuttal and accusation in September. In February 1737 the members of the town council, pragmatic as ever, noted that the 'incompetent' Krause would anyway be leaving the school by Easter, within two months; they severely advised both rector and cantor to observe to the letter the school regulations.[38]

Yet Bach could not let the matter lie. A week later he wrote again, restating all his grievances.[39] The town council seems to have made some further recommendations in April, but the details of their decision are not known. Bach wrote again on 21 August 1737 since he did not feel he had obtained 'satisfaction in respect to the humiliation to which I was subjected by the said Rector'.[40] In the end, he tried playing what he thought would be his trump card. He had recently received his title at the Dresden court, in November 1736; feeling strengthened by this, in October 1737 he wrote directly to the prince-elector, accusing Ernesti of 'effrontery'.[41] But the prince's decision in December 1737 was a cryptic Judgement of

Solomon, basically telling the Leipzig authorities to do whatever was necessary to solve the problem. It remains unclear exactly how the affair was finally settled, if at all. The violent antipathy between the two men continued until the end of Bach's life; in 1749 he was accused of being the author of an anonymous text that uses the word-play 'Dreckohr'/'Rektor' ('filthy ears'/'Rector').[42]

The Scheibe controversy (1737-1738)

Even before the dust had begun to settle with Ernesti, Bach found himself criticized in the press, but for a different reason. An anonymous article appeared in a Hamburg musical journal, the *Critischer Musikus*, edited by the organist Johann Adolph Scheibe, the son of the Leipzig organ builder whom Bach respected. Young Scheibe had moved to Hamburg, shortly after the cantor had been instrumental in not appointing him as Johann Gottlieb Görner's replacement in 1729. Not surprisingly, in Hamburg he fell under Telemann's influence, much admiring his simple style that was so immediately appealing.

Although Bach had voted against Scheibe in 1729, it is not absolutely sure that the young man's remarks – for he was indeed the anonymous author – were inspired by a spirit of vengeance. In fact, they were probably not even intended as especially strong criticisms at all. However, Bach was a susceptible man and was going through a particularly difficult period, owing to the conflict with Ernesti. The whole episode with Scheibe, like the one with the rector, soon got out of hand, although Bach did not participate directly.

Scheibe's first article appeared on 14 May 1737.[43] He praises Bach (without naming him) in generous terms as one of the most eminent of the *Musikanten*, justly famous for his extraordinary way of playing the harpsichord and the organ. Nevertheless, the second part of the article comments that Bach's works lack naturalness and are complicated, that their beauty is hidden by too much artifice, and that they are unnecessarily difficult. He adds that Bach unreasonably expects singers and instrumentalists to be able to perform what he can play with his own amazing fingers on the keyboard. Finally, he notes that Bach writes out much of the ornamentation, thereby smothering the melody and making it unrecognizable. Bach's art is artificial rather than natural, obscure rather than sublime; in sum, it is in 'conflict with Nature'.

Before we spring to Bach's defence, we should pause for a moment to remember just how unusual Bach's music is by comparison with that of all his important contemporaries in Germany, notably Telemann, but also Graun, as well as the leading composers at the Dresden Court, Hasse and Jan Dismas Zelenka. Our perspective can be distorted by Bach's uniquely complicated style. The music of these other composers can appear to lack some of the essential qualities present in Bach's music, including its intensity. This viewpoint is based on the assumption that it is less worthy to compose simple music that is easy to listen to. Such a value-judgement is even less tenable than Scheibe's.

Bach decided not to reply, but let several of his friends rise to his defence. The first was Johann Abraham Birnbaum (1702–48), a teacher of rhetoric at Leipzig University. His lengthy reply to Scheibe was published in January 1738, with a dedication to Bach.[44] Although Scheibe's article had been anonymous, Birnbaum lines up his arguments like so many arrows and makes it clear that he knows who his 'target' is. The German word for 'target' is *Scheibe*...He concedes that Bach's works are difficult to play but claims that Bach believes in a simple concept, an idea we have already seen in a quotation from Mattheson: 'that which I have achieved by industry and practice, anyone else with a tolerable natural gift and ability can also achieve...One can do anything if only one really wishes to, and if one industriously strives to convert natural abilities, by untiring zeal, into finished skills.'

Birnbaum rebukes Scheibe for using the pejorative and rather contemptuous word 'Musikanten', normally used to refer to relatively uneducated musicians, in connection with Bach. As for the criticism concerning the over-laden notation, covered in written-out ornamental figures, Birnbaum interestingly takes the view of modern scholars who point to Bach's stylistic indebtedness to French musical practice: 'From among a mass of composers I could cite in this respect, I will mention only Grigny and Du Mage, who in their *Livres d'orgue* have used this very method'.

Scheibe responded immediately, in February 1738, justifying his use in his first article of the word 'Musikanten'.[45] Did this touch a raw nerve with Bach, conscious of his lack of university education? Scheibe also poured scorn on how little Birnbaum, who was not really a musician, knew of 'the true basis of music or its real beauties'. Today, such claims seem weak, as if Scheibe had nothing more to say and was therefore hiding behind unassailable assertions of his own artistic superiority.

Another of Bach's learned university friends, Lorenz Christoph Mizler (1711–78), joined the fray the next year.[46] Scheibe replied again, this time using a pseudonym. He wrote a savage, if rather amusing, satire in which Bach (again unnamed) comes across as arrogant and preening.[47] Bach's supporters replied that this was 'not a permissible satire, but a shameful libel.'[48] Scheibe's last round came in 1745 when he reprinted Birnbaum's text with 164 footnotes and annotations, polemical and contentious from start to finish.[49]

During these difficult years the last of Johann Sebastian and Anna Magdalena's thirteen children were born: Johanna Carolina (*bapt.* 30 October 1737, *d.* 18 August 1781) and Regina Susanna (*bapt.* 22 February 1742, *d.* 14 December 1809). Carl Philipp Emanuel was named harpsichordist in Berlin to the Crown Prince Frederick (later Frederick the Great) in 1738. Bach visited him in Berlin in August 1741.

Side by side with these joys came further difficulties and sadness. Unfortunately, young Johann Gottfried Bernhard seems not to have been very stable. He had got severely into debt in Sangerhausen and run away. In May 1738 Bach wrote again to the authorities there. No longer did he see 'a Divine Decree' at work or 'Divine Providence' taking a hand. He wrote instead about 'my (alas! misguided) son', commenting 'I must bear my cross in patience, and leave my unruly son to God's Mercy alone, doubting not that He will hear my sorrowful pleading'. He goes on, about Holy Will, Divine Goodness, and the need for God's help and insists, somewhat defensively, 'I am fully confident that you will not impute the evil conduct of my child to me'. Nevertheless, he declines to pay his son's debts until they can be proven to him.[50]

Johann Gottfried Bernhard eventually turned up and tried to mend his ways. He enrolled as a law student at Jena University in 1739, but died on 27 May 1739, at the age of just 24.

Last Works (1739–50)

CLAVIER ÜBUNG III (1739)

In his last years Bach put more energy into publishing his best keyboard works. The third volume of *Clavier Übung*, a magnificent collection of organ music, contained his most significant homage to Luther. The heart of the volume is a series of 21 movements based on chorale tunes whose texts refer to and expound the central Lutheran doctrines. The melodies are developed musically in two ways, first at length, using a complex style, and then in a shorter and simpler manner. Bach thus consciously constructed a musical counterpart to, and illustration of, Luther's two famous doctrinal catechisms, one of which was long and the other short. This collection is unquestionably the finest volume of organ music printed in any country in the whole eighteenth century. It was published in Leipzig in 1739 for the 200th anniversary of the famous sermon preached in 1539 by Luther in the Thomaskirche.

Curiously, just before this homage to Luther Bach ran into trouble concerning a Passion performance, in Holy Week 1739. The reasons behind this are unknown, but there had evidently been another dispute, reminding us of the problem he had had with the town council over the performance of his first Passion, in 1723. Bach was now formally served notice forbidding him to perform a Passion. His reply, reported on 17 March 1739, gives a sharp insight into his state of mind, and the conditions in which he now worked. He 'did not care, for he got nothing out of it anyway, and it was only a burden'.[51]

THE 'GOLDBERG' VARIATIONS (1741–1742)

The catechism chorale preludes were followed two years later by a fourth volume of *Clavier Übung*, containing the 'Aria with 30 variations, for harpsichord with two manuals', BWV 988, now known as the 'Goldberg' Variations (although that title does not stem from Bach himself). The work was supposedly composed for the insomniac Hermann Carl von Keyserlingk, the Russian

Ambassador who had given Bach his letters of nomination to the title of Court Composer five years earlier. His son was a friend of Carl Philipp Emanuel's, and in 1741 was studying at Leipzig University. Bach went to Dresden in November 1741 and is known to have visited the Keyserlingk house. Yet if the work was indeed commissioned, why does Keyserlingk's name appear nowhere in the first edition?

As for the brilliant young virtuoso Johann Gottlieb Goldberg (1727–56), his name became attached to these variations perhaps because he was one of their first performers, but since the boy was only fourteen when they were published Bach is most unlikely to have written them for him, unless he had exceptionally long arms and large hands for his age, quite apart from the technical skills needed to play this most difficult of all Bach's harpsichord works.

Bach had now embarked on his last decade, a period during which he withdrew more and more from the problems of life at the Thomasschule and from the squabbles that had marked the previous fifteen years. Both he and Anna Magdalena were seriously ill at about this time, but recovered after some months of convalescence.[52] His two eldest sons were well established and on their way to becoming even more famous than he. They were already known as the 'Dresden Bach' (Wilhelm Friedemann) and the 'Berlin Bach' (Carl Philipp Emanuel). Johann Sebastian had become 'Old Bach'.

He now retreated increasingly into his own work and assembled the second volume of *The Well-Tempered Clavier*, BWV 870–893, considerably richer than the first, and the fruit of twenty years of maturity. Neither volume was published until 50 years after his death.

Some of his youthful organ chorales were revised at this time, notably a set of the finest ones composed in Weimar. They are now usually referred to as the 'Leipzig' Chorales, BWV 651–668. He also made organ arrangements of six chorale movements from his cantatas. These were engraved by the young Johann Georg Schübler, whose name has been attached to them ever since. They were published in about 1748 and have been among his most popular works ever since.

THE MUSICAL OFFERING (1747)

Embedded inside the 'Goldberg' Variations is a series of nine canons, complex compositions that are hard to write but sound deceptively simple, at least in Bach's hands. Canons also hold a central position in three other published works of his last years: the *Musical Offering* (1747), the five Canonic Variations on the chorale 'Vom Himmel hoch', BWV 769 (1747–8), and *The Art of Fugue* (1742–50). These great works are like a contrapuntal mountain range.

The *Musical Offering*, BWV 1079, is directly linked with the last journey that Bach made, to Potsdam (near Berlin), to visit Carl Philipp Emanuel. The story is well known but various accretions became attached to it during the eighteenth century. The simplest and oldest version is told by a Berlin newspaper on 11 May 1747.[53] Bach arrived on Sunday 7 May, after a long journey. News reached Frederick the Great that Old Bach was 'waiting in His Majesty's antechamber for His Majesty's most gracious permission to listen to the music'. The king gave Bach a 'royal theme', and asked him to improvise a fugue on it on one of the new fortepianos built by Gottfried Silbermann. Bach did so, and promised to write the fugue down on paper and have it printed. On the Monday evening, 'His Majesty charged him again with the execution of a fugue, in six parts, which he accomplished just as skilfully as on the previous occasion, to the pleasure of His Majesty and to the general admiration'.

Bach's two eldest sons were witnesses of the scene. According to Carl Philipp Emanuel (seven years later, in 1754),[54] the request for a fugue with 'six real voices' occurred at the same time as the first fugue. He confirms that the engraved *Musical Offering* that Bach sent contained the two fugues, in three parts and in six parts, both with the title 'Ricercar', as well as 'several other intricate little pieces' based on the king's theme. In Wilhelm Friedemann's version (as recounted by Forkel in 1802),[55] Frederick the Great announced Bach's arrival to the assembled musicians with the words 'Gentlemen, Old Bach is come!' And it was Bach who asked for a theme. Then the king, 'probably to see how far such art could be carried, expressed a wish to hear also a Fugue with six obbligato parts. But as not every subject is fit for such full harmony, Bach chose one himself.'

Whether the event took place on one or two evenings, the result was the same. Bach improvised a three-part fugue and promised to engrave it, then later improvised a six-part fugal work. Two months later, on 7 July 1747, after having had two fugues based on the royal theme engraved by Johann Georg Schübler,[56] he sent the king his *Musical Offering.*

Bach sent only the first instalment at this stage. He added a general title in the form of a Latin acrostic on the word 'Ricercar' (an old word for fugue): **Regis Iussu Cantio Et Reliqua Canonica Arte Resoluta**, or 'the music asked for by the king, and the remainder worked out in canonic art'. He later added a magnificent trio sonata based on the royal theme and a group of 'diverse canons on the royal theme'. The full work was not ready until September 1747.

The historical circumstances surrounding the *Musical Offering* suggest that the three-part ricercar is one of Bach's rare works that was deliberately conceived for the fortepiano rather than the harpsichord; it is in the most modern style, and is well suited to the modern instrument. On the other hand, the six-part ricercar is in the old style; it was undoubtedly intended for the old instrument, the harpsichord. Bach printed 100 copies. One year later he wrote to his cousin that he had none left, having given most of them away.[57]

The whole work, as Christoph Wolff has suggested, may be seen as a musical 'self-portrait of Bach' in his three different roles as keyboard virtuoso and master of the fugue (the two ricercars), *Capellmeister* and chamber musician (the trio sonata), and learned composer and contrapuntist (the ten canons).[58]

THE CANONIC VARIATIONS (1747–1748)
Bach's last works are marked by a unique style that owes nothing to fashion. Most of the works of the 1740s, whose style is announced by the 'Goldberg' Variations, have staggeringly complex forms, hidden like inner scaffolding. Their structural designs are admirable intellectual achievements. Yet these compositions also have a much simpler outer surface, a musical language that is less complex harmonically than many of Bach's earlier works.

The second of the late 'contrapuntal peaks' was linked to Bach's joining the select Society for Musical Sciences. This had been founded in 1738 (and would be disbanded in 1755). Lorenz Christoph Mizler, its secretary, was an old student of Johann

Matthias Gesner, the former rector of the Thomasschule who had been a friend of Bach's. Mizler had studied the keyboard with Bach and considered him his 'good friend and patron'; he had already taken up his pen in 1739 to defend his teacher against Scheibe.

Bach joined as the fourteenth member in June 1747. Other members included Telemann (sixth member, 1739), Handel (eleventh member, 1745) and Graun (thirteenth member, 1746).[59] Fourteen was Bach's number since, according to the old system whereby A = 1, B = 2, C = 3, and so on, B + A + C + H (2 + 1 + 3 + 8) = 14. At about the same time he added precisely fourteen canons (BWV 1087) by hand at the back of his own printed copy of the 'Goldberg' Variations.

One of the rules of Mizler's society obliged members to submit a published 'scientific' work every year until the age of 65. Bach's first contribution, in June 1747, was the little volume containing the 'Vom Himmel hoch' Variations for organ, BWV 769, an astonishing display of learned canonic art.[60] For his second contribution, in June 1748, he may have sent members copies of the *Musical Offering*, learnedly printed in open score and with its elaborate canons. (This would help explain why he had none left when his cousin asked for a copy that year.[61]) Bach knew that he would only have to provide one further contribution to the members, in June 1749, since by June 1750 he would be already 65 and over the age limit for submitting such works.

Bach printed his 'scientific' variations in cryptic fashion, forcing his colleagues to work before they could play them. Those who made the effort discovered one of the most sparkling, playful works he had ever composed.

In 1754, Johann Michael Schmidt referred with admiration to these canons: 'I cannot persuade myself that the most difficult demonstration in geometry requires much deeper and more extensive reflection than this labour must have demanded'.[62] But Bach enjoyed hiding his esoteric skills behind a facade of great simplicity. Friedrich Wilhelm Marpurg referred in 1760 to 'old Bach, who (so to speak) shook all sort of paper intricacies out of his sleeve, any one of which would make many a man sweat for days, and most likely in vain'[63] and Forkel noted approvingly that 'a great amount of canonic artifice is introduced in the most unconstrained manner'.[64]

All these authors understood that for Bach at the end of his life *ars est artem celare*, the true skill is to hide the skill. In most of these late canonic works, Bach hides the monumental skill behind a bubbling fountain of good-natured music. Composing them must have been as relaxing for him as doing a crossword puzzle.

On the title-page of the third volume of *Clavier Übung* Bach had stated that his music was composed 'for Music Lovers and especially for Connoisseurs of such work, to refresh their Spirits'. To write the variations on 'Vom Himmel hoch' required unique skill and to understand them fully today requires the knowledge of 'connoisseurs'. But to appreciate them only requires ears and the ability to sit and relax for fifteen minutes of pure pleasure.

Just before joining Mizler's society, Bach had sat, for rather longer than fifteen minutes, to have his portrait painted by Elias Gottlob Haussmann (1695–1774), the official painter to the Leipzig town council. The earliest-known version of this famous portrait is dated 1746.[65] Bach is shown holding a puzzle canon now known to be one of the fourteen he copied in at the back of his own copy of the 'Goldberg' Variations. One of the conditions imposed on members of Mizler's society was that 'each member should at his convenience send a picture of himself, well painted on canvas, to the library, where it will be retained as a memento'. The best Bach portrait that survives is an excellent replica of Haussmann's painting, dated 1748. It has been in a private collection in the USA since 1953.[66]

The Art of Fugue (1742–1750)

Bach's last keyboard works are all different from his earlier ones. They are monothematic, being unified throughout all the movements by the presence of a single theme. *The Art of Fugue*, BWV 1080, contains fourteen (again!) fugues based on a single theme. He probably started work on this collection in about 1742.

Although he did not live to see it through the press, *The Art of Fugue* may possibly have been intended as a fifth and final volume of *Clavier Übung*. There is no doubt at all about it being keyboard music, despite the many erroneous legends that have arisen during the twentieth century and the vast number of arrangements that have unjustifiably been made of it. It is one of his most expressive harpsichord works.

Bach may also have intended it as his third and final 'scientific' offering to his colleagues of the Mizler society, for June 1749, but things went wrong because he became ill. *The Art of Fugue* was engraved by Johann Heinrich Schübler, the younger brother of Johann Georg Schübler who had engraved the *Musical Offering* and the 'Schübler' Chorales.[67] Bach's original idea was to include fourteen movements, twelve fugues and two canons. He copied out a fair version of these pieces in about 1745. At some point he changed his mind and wrote two more fugues, bringing their number to fourteen. He also added two more canons. When the engraving was half-completed he interrupted the process and started changing the order.

The idea for such a work may have been slowly germinating all his life, ever since the visit to Buxtehude in 1705. Did he remember the learned work that Buxtehude had written on his father's death in 1674, containing two four-part pieces in D minor with the Latin title *Contrapunctus* ('counterpoint')? Bach now returned to this same idea at the end of his life for *The Art of Fugue*, but transformed it beyond recognition. The fugues are all called *Contrapunctus*, and are all in D minor. Almost all are in four voices, and the contrapuntal writing is refined beyond anything Bach himself had yet achieved. It is the most exalted of all the peaks in his contrapuntal mountain range.

Although Bach must have finished it, *The Art of Fugue* remains unfinished for posterity. Somehow, the ending got lost. As he worked on it the fourteenth and last fugue turned into an enormous composition, one of his longest. Bach clearly allowed six pages for it in the carefully worked-out engraving plan (as Gregory Butler has shown),[68] but when the last page of his manuscript disappeared, after his death, the order of the pieces was arbitrarily changed by his inheritors, destroying his plan and creating a confusion that has lasted for 250 years.

The B minor Mass (*c*.1749)

The Art of Fugue is usually said to be Bach's last work, and with good reason since it is generally thought that he died while working on the last fugue. However, there is one other great work that he finished in the last years of his life, the B minor Mass, BWV 232. In his later years Bach had become fascinated by the contrapuntal art of earlier composers, notably Palestrina. He seems to have wanted to leave a final religious work that would be a summary of many of the different kinds of writing styles he had developed during his lifetime. In 1733, he had sent to Dresden the first two movements, the Kyrie and Gloria. The Credo was possibly assembled as late as 1747–8, drawing partly on the music for movements from cantatas he had written during the previous thirty years, in Weimar and Leipzig (BWV 12, 120 and 171), but adding much new material. For the Sanctus, he took over the splendid work he had written in 1724, for his second Christmas in Leipzig, and had performed on several other occasions over the years. For the Osanna he adapted one of his secular cantatas that he had written in 1732 for the prince-elector's name day; as with the *Christmas Oratorio*, putting secular music to sacred use was not a problem for him.

The Agnus Dei was put together by adapting a movement from BWV 11, a cantata he had written for Ascension Day in 1735, and by using again the 'Gratias agimus' from the Gloria to provide a 'Dona nobis pacem'. The words ask for peace, but Bach's music builds to a final blaze of glory as the high 'clarino' trumpets soar above the choir and orchestra.

The roots of 'late Bach' may be found in 'early Bach'. Or, to put it another way, many of his most characteristic features, both musically and personally, are present at the start of his life and come to the front again at the end. The 'Goldberg' Variations (1741–2) link with the chorale partitas for organ (1700–05). The 'Vom Himmel hoch' Variations (1747) are based on the same theme as one of his earliest organ works, BWV 738 (1707–08). The Crucifixus of the B minor Mass (1748–9) is taken from the cantata *Weinen, Klagen, Sorgen, Zagen* (1714). Even *The Art of Fugue* had roots that can be traced back to his youthful visit to Lübeck, nearly half a century earlier.

Although there is an impressive uniformity of language and musical discourse to all his works, no two pieces are interchangeable. His capacity for concentration and his enforced habits of having to work at high speed did not lead to facility, as it did with some of his contemporaries. He was saved from such a fate by the very characteristics that entangled him in so many conflicts with colleagues since his impatience and his pride would not allow him to repeat himself.

'Quaerendo invenietis'

Several of Bach's occasional canons were dedicated to friends. The first, BWV 1073, is dated 2 August 1713, and may have been dedicated to Johann Gottfried Walther.[1] A more enigmatic one, BWV 1074, was dedicated to 'Monsieur Houdemann' (the lawyer Ludwig Friedrich Hudemann) and engraved in Leipzig in about 1727; it has two different solutions.[2] A third, BWV 1075, was copied out by the composer 'as a memento for his good friend'; it is dated 10 January 1734.[3]

The composition of such canons was thus a gesture of musical friendship. These little pieces were usually written out in cryptic form, like a musical riddle. Bach humorously acknowledges the work involved in the Musical Offering canons by adding the Latin phrase 'Quaerendo invenietis': 'By seeking, you will find'.

Bach's last canon and possibly his last composition, BWV 1078, is dated 1 March 1749. It is a particularly complex little work for seven canonic parts plus an eighth voice. The Latin text contains a friendly acrostic on the names 'Faber' and 'Bach'.[4]

The canon seems to have been dedicated to Benjamin Gottlob Faber. He must have been a good friend since Bach wrote that 'to remember a friend means happiness':

Fidelis Amici Beatum Esse Recordari.

The composer's own name is referred to in the phrase '[in Bach] you have someone who cultivates good art':

Bonae Artis Cultorem Habeas.

CHAPTER FIVE

28 July 1750

Come, sweet Death, come, happy Rest!
Come, lead me in joy
For I am tired of the world…

BWV 478, Song 59 from Schemelli's Gesang-Buch, 1736

Handel and Bach had more in common than music and their joint membership of the Mizler society. An announcement published in Berlin in April 1750 by a London eye surgeon, John Taylor, states that he had just operated on the celebrated '*Capellmeister* Bach who, by the frequent use he had made of his eyes, had almost lost his sight'.[1] This operation seems to have taken place between March 28 and April 1. Taylor later recounted, in 1761, that he had operated on 'a celebrated master of music' in Leipzig in early 1750, and claimed that the operation for cataracts had been a complete success.[2] This was not true. A second operation was equally unsuccessful since in May 1750 one witness noted Bach was 'still suffering from much inflammation and other troubles'.[3] Some years later Taylor operated on Handel, with the same disastrous results.

Carl Philipp Emanuel suggests that the damage may have been done when Bach was very young, copying out his older brother's volume of organ music by candlelight at night, a comment that implies that his father's eyesight was weak all his life. In his father's obituary (1754) he notes that 'the operation, although it had to be repeated, turned out very badly.'[4]

According to Bach's pupil Kirnberger, Bach had the habit of saying 'It ought to be possible to do everything' ('es muss alles möglich zu machen seyn').[5] Now it had become almost impossible to do anything. By late May 1749 most of Bach's family and friends, as well as his employers, understood that he could not live for long. He was almost blind and in poor health. Count von Brühl, the prime minister in Dresden, wrote a letter to the Leipzig authorities on 2 June 1749, recommending the director of music in his chapel, Gottlieb Harrer (1703–55), as the new cantor 'upon the eventual occasion of the decease of Mr Bach'.[6] On 8 June, Harrer gave a trial performance with one of his own compositions, in the presence of many town dignitaries.

Bach was not yet dead, however, although by this stage it had probably become impossible for him to fulfil most of his duties. That the Leipzig authorities should have moved to replace him while Bach was still alive, acting as if he were already dead, seems particularly lacking in tact. Carl Philipp Emanuel comments that 'Not only could he no longer use his eyes, but his whole system, which was otherwise thoroughly healthy, was completely overthrown by the operation and by the harmful medicaments and other things' and that Bach was 'almost continuously ill for full half a year.'[7]

Not long after the operations, probably in May 1750, Bach recovered sufficiently to take in briefly a last student, the brilliant young Johann Gottfried Müthel (1728–88). He also rallied sufficiently to correspond with a colleague until 26 May 1750 and get embroiled in a final dispute, this time with the organist Christoph Gottlieb Schröter (1699–1782), a member of the Mizler society.

About 40 years earlier, back in his Weimar days, Bach had commented to his cousin Walther that the famous family name could be used melodically: 'B, A, C, H', in German notation, corresponds to the chromatic theme B♭, A, C, B♮.[8] He now used his own name for the first time in all his works, as the final theme in the closing bars of the last fugue of *The Art of Fugue*. By using these four notes as the last theme in the fourteenth fugue, Bach signed his last pun, no doubt thinking to bring down the curtain elegantly. He had come full circle and had completed his life's work. Yet circumstances beyond his control cheated him, posthumously, of this supremely elegant ending.

In the confusion after his death, perhaps because his inheritors were in a hurry to publish the work, the last page seems to have been lost. The fourteenth fugue was left incomplete, although Bach had surely finished it. *The Art of Fugue* breaks off in the middle of a phrase, one of the most startling moments in all the history of music. Carl Philipp Emanuel wrote on the manuscript underneath these notes 'Here, where the name B.A.C.H. occurs as a counter-subject, the composer died'.[9] In posterity's eyes, Old Bach's sublime farewell had been transformed into high drama. His serene final fugue had been violently interrupted, by silence.

Ten months after his death, *The Art of Fugue*, Bach's musical testament, was finally published, but incomplete. As a compensation for the unfinished state of the last piece, purchasers were given a supplement in the form of a chorale in four voices added at the end 'which the deceased in his blindness dictated ex tempore to one of his friends.'[10] This is 'Wenn wir in höchsten Nöten sein'. The melody is derived from *Lève le coeur, ouvre l'oreille* by Louis Bourgeois (1547).

Some of his own works had already been inspired by this tune, which had been the basis for Pachelbel's choral work that he may have sung in Lüneburg. Bach himself had already used it in BWV 641, a particularly beautiful and introspective little piece in the *Orgel-Büchlein* with highly elaborate ornamentation recalling Buxtehude's chorales. The work printed in *The Art of Fugue*, BWV 668a, is a reworking of the *Orgel-Büchlein* chorale.

All three lower voices, the accompaniment, are left basically untouched, but in the chorale melody all the ornamentation is stripped away, leaving the original theme bare. And in a gesture of expressive contrapuntal artistry – as undemonstrative as it is admirable – serene fugal introductions are added before the statement of each line of the chorale.

Bach's death-bed dictation would seem to be a touching legend since he had already included this version in the manuscript collection of chorales he had revised in Leipzig, some years earlier. Yet there must have been some link. Perhaps he asked to hear the piece? At any rate, he did now alter the title. Although the opening line of the first verse ('When we are in greatest need') could have seemed appropriate to his suffering, he now made a significant change, replacing this by the opening line of another hymn sung to the same tune: 'I humbly stand before thy throne, O God'. A mood of profound peace and resignation permeates the whole work.

Even though Bach was now blind, normal daylight hurt his eyes so he covered them with a black bandage. He briefly recovered his sight one morning, on about 18 July. He had a stroke a few hours later, 'followed by a raging fever'.[11] Two of the finest physicians in Leipzig attended him during this period. On 22 July, the eighth Sunday after Trinity, he received communion, in private, a certain sign that his death was imminent.[12] The end finally came, six days later, on Tuesday 28 July 1750, at around a quarter past eight in the evening.[13]

Shortly afterwards, the event was noted by his old friend and colleague, Abraham Kriegel, as follows: 'This 28 July, in the afternoon, at about 8 o'clock, Mr Johann Sebastian Bach, Composer to the Court of His Majesty the King of Poland and Serene Highness Prince-Elector in Saxony, honorary Capellmeister of His Serene Highness the Prince of Anhalt-Cöthen and of His Serene Highness the Prince of Saxe-Weissenfels, as well as Director of Music and Cantor at St Thomas's School, has left this earth. The fatal complications of an eye operation have taken from the world this man who, by his extraordinary musical art, has achieved an immortal glory...'[14]

No-one was really surprised by his death and the town council, not wasting any time, met the next day to choose Bach's successor. Without seriously considering the merits of the other four men (who included Carl Philipp Emanuel), the ten members voted unanimously for the insignificant Harrer since he had the all-important support of the prime minister. He had studied at Leipzig University and was also 'a master of both the Latin and Greek languages'.[15] The other candidates 'were all skilled musicians, to be sure, but whether they were capable of [giving] the instruction was to be doubted.'[16] Nothing had really changed since 1723. A last remark from the honourable Dr Stieglitz, a military man, sums up Bach's life in Leipzig. It throws into sharp perspective the everyday reality of his uphill struggle for 27 years: 'Mr. Bach had been a great musician, it is true, but not a school-teacher'.[17]

Nevertheless, the announcement that was read from the pulpit of the Thomaskirche three days after his death was respectful: 'The Esteemed and Highly Respected Mr Johann Sebastian Bach...has peacefully and blissfully departed in God...His dead body was this day in accordance with Christian usage committed to the earth.'[18] Bach was buried in the cemetery of the Johanniskirche, outside the Leipzig town walls. The entry in the death register is even more sober: 'A man, 67 years, Mr Johann Sebastian Bach, Capellmeister and Cantor of the Thomasschule, died Tuesday.' (This mistakenly ages Bach by two years, since he was only 65.) The oak coffin, made by a Mr Müller, cost 4 thalers. The fee for the burial was 2 thalers, 14 groschen, but there was no charge for the hearse.[19]

Apparently Bach left no will. An inventory of his estate was drawn up for the inheritors in the autumn of 1750.[20] The total came to 1122 thalers, 16 groschen. He had debts and 'other necessary expenses' totalling almost 154 thalers, including the 2 thalers and 16 groschen owed to young Johann Heinrich Schübler for finishing off the engraving of *The Art of Fugue*. His total assets came to 968 thalers, little more than one year's salary. The family owned no property. There was one share in a mine (60 thalers), and some gold, silver, petty cash and medals (292 thalers). There was a surprisingly large amount of household silverware (251 thalers). The books were almost entirely religious (38 thalers). The nineteen musical instruments (5 harpsichords, 2 *lautenwercks*, 1 little spinet, 3 violins, 3 violas, 1 little bass, 2 cellos, 1 viola da gamba, 1 lute) accounted for one third of the whole estate, at 371 thalers, 16 groschen. The youngest son, Johann Christian, had already been given three 'keyboards' with a set of pedals. This may refer to a double clavichord with pedals, plus another separate instrument. Bach's personal effects included eleven shirts, a silver dagger (12 thalers), a stick with a silver top, a pair of silver shoe-buckles. There were three coats, one of which was for funerals.

He was buried (according to an oral tradition) in a 'flat grave' situated 'six paces from the south wall' of the Johanniskirche.[21] An engraving by Joachim Ernst Scheffer dating from 1749, just one year before his funeral, clearly shows the graveyard and the south side of the church (near the present Grassi Museum).[22] A visitor in 1800 (J. F. Rochlitz) commented that his tomb could no longer be identified[23] and in 1833 the cemetery was closed and abandoned.

Schumann was horrified to find that the grave was not marked and Mendelssohn gave an organ recital to raise funds for a memorial slab.[24]

On 22 October 1894, more than half a century later, three oak coffins were found in about the right spot. One contained the bones of a young woman; another had a skeleton with a broken skull. The third contained the bones of an 'elderly man, not very large, but well-built'. The skull, with its prominent jaw bone, high forehead, deep-set eye sockets and marked nasal angle, was compatible with the famous portrait of Bach painted by Haussmann in 1746. The skeleton was therefore identified by the anatomist Wilhelm His (using means that modern science would no doubt find rather summary) as being very probably that of Bach. The capacity of the skull was 1479.5 cc, and the length of the bones suggested that the height of the body had been about 167 cm.[25] On 16 July 1900 'Bach' was reburied in a new oak coffin in a vault under the altar inside the Johanniskirche. The church was destroyed by allied bombing during the Second World War, on 4 December 1943, but the replacement coffin was later identified.

Johann Sebastian Bach was again reburied, this time in the Thomaskirche, on 28 July 1949, the 199th anniversary of his death. In 1964 the tomb was moved again to its present position, inside the chancel. Although there is no absolute certainty that the body is Johann Sebastian Bach's, its presence there is more than symbolic. It makes the Thomaskirche the uncontested centre of all Bach pilgrimages. Even visitors who are aware of the doubts about the identification of the body and who are uncomfortable with musical hagiography cannot leave the church unmoved.

Bibliographical References and Notes

Most of the quotations from seventeenth- and eighteenth-century sources may be found in the *Bach-Dokumente* in the original German text. A selection of these appears in *The New Bach Reader* (the translation given here is usually the same; it is used with permission of the publishers). Quotations from Johann Nicolaus Forkel use the English translation in *On Johann Sebastian Bach's Life, Genius and Works* (1820) which was almost certainly made by A. C. F. Kollmann. It is reprinted in *The Bach Reader*.

Principal sources:

B-Dok   *Bach-Dokumente*, 3 vols., ed. Werner Neumann and Hans-Joachim Schulze (Basel, Bärenreiter, 1963–84)

BEST   *Bach en son temps*, ed. Gilles Cantagrel (Paris, Hachette, 1982; revised edition, Paris, Fayard, 1997)

Bild   Werner Neumann, *Bilddokumente zur Lebensgeschichte Johann Sebastian Bachs* (Basel, Bärenreiter, 1979)

BR   *The Bach Reader: A Life of Johann Sebastian Bach in Letters and Documents*, ed. Hans T. David and Arthur Mendel, revised edition with supplement (New York, Norton, 1966). See also *NBR*.

BWV   *Bach-Werke-Verzeichnis, Kleine Ausgabe*, ed. Alfred Dürr and Yoshitake Kobayashi (Wiesbaden, Breitkopf, 1998) [the revised BWV catalogue]

MGG   *Die Musik in Geschichte und Gegenwart*, 17 vols., ed. Friedrich Blume (Munich, Deutschen Taschenbuch Verlage, 1949–86)

NBR   *The New Bach Reader*, revised and enlarged by Christoph Wolff (New York and London, Norton, 1998)

NG   *The New Grove Dictionary of Music and Musicians*, 20 vols., ed. Stanley Sadie (London, Macmillan, 1980), notably the articles by Christoph Wolff, Walter Emery, Richard Jones and Eugene Helm on Johann Sebastian and other members of the Bach family; also many other relevant articles

Notes

Chapter One
Son, Orphan, Brother, Organ Student
(1685–1703)

1 *B-Dok*, vol. 3, no. 927, p. 444; *NBR*, no. 396, p. 404; *BR*, p. 283; *BEST*, p. 406.

2 Bach lists 53 in his 1735 Genealogy. *NG* gives details of about 80. Karl Geiringer and Irene Geiringer, *The Bach Family: Seven Generations of Creative Genius* (New York, 1954) discusses 92 musical Bachs.

3 *Discovering and Experiencing Eisenach: 90 years of the Bach House* (Eisenach, Kulturamt Eisenach, 1995), p. 4; Jost Schilgen, *Eisenach* (Grasberg, Sachbuchverlag, 1997), p. 42.

4 *Der Volkommene Capellmeister*, 1739, p. 144; *B-Dok*, vol. 2, no. 464, p. 374; *BEST*, p. 276.

5 Letter from C. P. E. Bach to Forkel, 13 January 1775: *B-Dok*, vol. 3, no. 803, p. 288; *NBR*, no. 395, pp. 398–9; *BR*, p. 278; *BEST*, p. 488.

6 *NBR*, p. 478; *BR*, p. 352; *BEST*, p. 599.

7 Letter from C. P. E. Bach to Forkel, 13 January 1775: *B-Dok*, vol. 3, no. 803, p. 289; *NBR*, no. 395, p. 399; *BR*, p. 279; *BEST*, p. 489.

8 Blaise Pascal, Fragment 41, *Pensées*, ed. Michel Le Guern, vol. 1 (Paris, Gallimard, 1977), p. 41.

9 On Johann Ambrosius, see Claus Oefner, *Die Musikerfamilie Bach in Eisenach, Schriften zur Musikgeschichte Thüringens*, vol. 1 (Eisenach, 1996), pp. 15–28.

10 On Johann Christoph, see Oefner, *op. cit.*, pp. 44–62. J. S. Bach's comment: *B-Dok*, vol. 1, no. 184,

p. 258; *NBR*, no. 303, p. 288; *BR*, p. 206; *BEST*, p. 30. C. P. E. Bach's comment: *B-Dok*, vol. 3, no. 666, p. 80; *NBR*, no. 306, p. 298; *BR*, p. 215; *BEST*, p. 468.

11 *NG*, vol. 14, p. 46.

12 *NG*, vol. 1, p. 775.

13 *B-Dok*, vol. 2, no. 3; *NBR*, no. 7, p. 33; *BR*, p. 427; *BEST*, p. 42.

14 Beethoven seems to have been the first to note that Bach was not a 'stream' but an 'ocean' ('Meer'). See *NBR*, p. 490.

15 1754 obituary: *B-Dok*, vol. 3, no. 666, p. 81; *NBR*, no. 306, p. 299; *BR*, p. 216; *BEST*, p. 469. Forkel: *NBR*, p. 425; *BR*, p. 301; *BEST*, p. 510.

16 1754 obituary: *B-Dok*, vol. 3, no. 666, pp. 81–2; *NBR*, no. 306, p. 299; *BR*, pp. 216–17; *BEST*, p. 469. Forkel: *NBR*, p. 425; *BR*, pp. 301–2; *BEST*, pp. 510–11.

17 *Bild*, nos. 30–4, pp. 366, 410.

18 *Bild*, no. 31, pp. 57, 366, 410.

19 Konrad Küster, *Der junge Bach* (Stuttgart, Deutsche Verlags-Anstalt, 1996), pp. 110–11.

20 1754 obituary: *B-Dok*, vol. 3, no. 666, p. 82; *NBR*, no. 306, pp. 299–300; *BR*, p. 217; *BEST*, p. 470.

21 Letter from C. P. E. Bach to Forkel, 13 January 1775: *B-Dok*, vol. 3, no. 803, p. 288; *NBR*, no. 395, p. 398 (mistranslated); *BR*, p. 278 (mistranslated); *BEST*, p. 488.

22 *B-Dok*, vol. 2, no. 224, p. 169; *BEST* p. 169.

23 *NG*, vol. 8, p. 66; *NG*, vol. 9, pp. 844, 847.

24 *B-Dok*, vol. 3, no. 739, p. 192; *NBR*, no. 358, p. 364; *BR*, p. 258; *BEST*, p. 115.

25 *NBR*, p. 474; *BR*, p. 348; *BEST*, p. 592.
26 *B-Dok*, vol. 2, no. 14, pp. 16–18; *NBR*, no. 19, pp. 43–6; *BR*, p. 51; *BEST*, pp. 50–53.
27 *NBR*, no. 256, pp. 233–4; *BEST*, p. 307; [*B-Dok*, vol. 1, no. 45c].

'Ein starker Appetit...'
1 *B-Dok*, vol. 3, no. 914, pp. 423–4; *NBR*, no. 397, p. 409; *BR*, p. 288; *BEST*, pp. 44–5.
2 *B-Dok*, vol. 2, no. 21; *NBR*, no. 22b, pp. 49–50; *BR*, p. 54; *BEST*, p. 59; Küster, *Der junge Bach*, p. 154.
3 Küster, *op. cit.*, p. 186.
4 *B-Dok*, vol. 1, no. 5, pp. 25–6; *B-Do*k, vol I, no. 85, pp. 157–9; *B-Dok*, vol. 1, no. 108, p. 188. *B-Dok*, vol. 2, no. 76, pp. 59–61; *B-Dok*, vol. 2, no. 78, p. 62; *NBR*, nos. 58–61, pp. 73–7; *BR*, pp. 71–4; *BEST*, pp. 85–91.
5 *NBR*, no. 60, p. 77; *BR*, p. 74; *BEST*, p. 92.
6 *B-Dok*, vol. 1, no. 44, pp. 110–11; *NBR*, no. 221, pp. 211–12; *BR*, p. 168; *BEST*, p. 280.

Chapter Two
Organist and Court Composer
(1703–1717)
1 *B-Dok*, vol. 3, no. 820, p. 315; *NBR*, no. 404, p. 412; *BR*, p. 291.
2 1754 obituary: *B-Dok*, vol. 3, no. 666, p. 82; *NBR*, no. 306, p. 300; *BR*, p. 217; *BEST*, p. 470.
3 Küster, *Der junge Bach*, p. 119; *Bild*, no. 46, pp. 66, 367, 410; *NBR*, no. 13, p. 39.
4 *Bild*, no. 44, p. 65.
5 *B-Dok*, vol. 2, no. 7, p. 10; *NBR*, no. 15, p. 40; *BR*, p. 49; *BEST*, p. 46; Küster, *Der junge Bach*, p. 119.
6 *Bild*, no. 56, pp. 70, 367, 411.
7 *B-Dok*, vol. 2, no. 7; *NBR*, no. 15, p. 40; *BR*, p. 49; *BEST*, p. 46.
8 *B-Dok*, vol. 2, no. 8; *NBR*, no. 16, p. 41; *BR*, pp. 49–50; *BEST*, pp. 47–8.
9 *B-Dok*, vol. 1, no. 94, p. 180; *NBR*,

no. 17a, p. 42.
10 Küster, *Der junge Bach*, pp. 124–9.
11 *Bild*, no. 48, pp. 67, 367, 411.
12 1754 obituary: *B-Dok*, vol. 3, no. 666, p. 82; *NBR*, no. 306, p. 300; *BR*, p. 217; *BEST*, p. 470.
13 *Répertoire International des Sources Musicales* (*RISM*) A/I/6, P 36. See Pachelbel's preface.
14 *NG*, vol. 11, p. 833.
15 Gary C. Thomas, '"Was George Frideric Handel gay?": on closet questions and cultural politics', *Queering the Pitch: the New Gay and Lesbian Musicology*, ed. Philip Brett, Elizabeth Wood and Gary C. Thomas (New York, Routledge, 1994), pp. 157–71.
16 *NG*, vol. 3, p. 527; *NG*, vol. 16, p. 642.
17 Peter Williams, *The Organ Music of J. S. Bach*, vol. 3 (Cambridge, Cambridge University Press, 1980–84), p. 122 (footnote); see also *NG*, vol. 3, p. 530.
18 *Bild*, no. 68, pp. 77, 368, 411.
19 *RISM* A/I/1, B 5204–5.
20 *RISM* A/I/1, B 5200.
21 1754 obituary: *B-Dok*, vol. 3, no. 666, p. 82; *NBR*, no. 306, p. 300; *BR*, p. 218; *BEST*, p. 471.
22 *B-Dok*, vol. 2, no. 16; *NBR*, no. 20, p. 46; *BR*, pp. 51–2; *BEST*, p. 54.
23 Philip Brett, 'Musicality, essentialism, and the closet', *Queering the Pitch: the New Gay and Lesbian Musicology*, ed. Philip Brett, Elizabeth Wood and Gary C. Thomas (New York, Routledge, 1994), p. 14.
24 *B-Dok*, vol. 2, no. 17; *NBR*, no. 21, p. 48; *BR*, p. 53; *BEST*, p. 57.
25 *NG*, vol. 1, pp. 788–9.
26 *B-Dok*, vol. 2, no. 21, p. 24; *NBR*, no. 22–5, pp. 49–51; *BR*, pp. 54–5; *BEST*, pp. 59–60.
27 *Bild*, nos. 82–4, pp. 83, 368, 412.
28 *Bild*, no. 91, pp. 87, 368–9, 412.
29 *B-Dok*, vol. 1, no. 83, pp. 152–5; *NBR*, no. 31, pp. 55–6; *BR*,

pp. 58–60; *BEST*, pp. 62–4.

30 *B-Dok*, vol. 1, no. 1, pp. 19–20;
    NBR, no. 32, p. 57; *BR*, pp. 60–61;
    BEST, pp. 66–7.

31 *B-Dok*, vol. 2, no. 36, p. 33; *NBR*,
    no. 33, p. 58; *BR*, p. 61; *BEST*, p. 69.

32 *MGG*, vol. 1, col. 920; Küster, *Der
    junge Bach*, pp. 126–7, 182–3.

33 Küster, *op. cit.*, pp. 186–7; *NBR*,
    no. 35, p. 59.

34 *MGG*, vol. 3, cols. 795–6; *NG*,
    vol. 5, p. 628.

35 *B-Dok*, vol. 2, no. 73; *NBR*, no. 57,
    p. 73; *BEST*, p. 84.

36 *B-Dok*, vol. 2, no. 53, p. 71; *NBR*,
    no. 53, p. 71; *BR*, p. 69.

37 *Bild*, nos. 102–3, pp. 93–4, 369,
    412; Küster, *Der junge Bach*,
    p. 187; *NBR*, no. 51, p. 70.

38 *NBR*, no. 39, p. 61–3; *BR*, pp. 62–3.

39 1754 obituary: *B-Dok*, vol. 3,
    no. 666, pp. 82–3; *NBR*, no. 306,
    p. 300; *BR*, p. 218; *BEST*, p. 471.

40 Forkel: *NBR*, p. 435; *BR*, p. 310;
    BEST, pp. 524–5.

41 *B-Dok*, vol. 1, nos. 1, 4, 65; *B-Dok*,
    vol. 2, no. 63, p. 50; *NBR*,
    nos. 46–50, pp. 65–70; *BR*, pp. 65–8;
    BEST, pp. 76–81.

42 *B-Dok*, vol. 2, nos. 66, 73, pp. 52,
    57; *NBR*, nos. 51, 57, pp. 70, 73;
    BR, pp. 67, 71; *BEST*, pp. 82, 84.

43 *NG*, vol. 20, p. 192.

44 *NBR*, nos. 70a, 87, pp. 82, 93; *BR*,
    pp. 76, 89.

45 *B-Dok*: 1754 obituary, vol. 3,
    no. 666, pp. 83–4; other accounts,
    vol. 2, nos. 441, 675, 696, 811a, 914.
    NBR: obituary, no. 306, pp. 300–03;
    other accounts, nos. 67, 396,
    pp. 79–80, 408; Forkel, p. 427. *BR*:
    obituary, pp. 218–19; other
    accounts, pp. 287, 444, 452–3;
    Forkel, pp. 303–4. *BEST*: obituary,
    pp. 471–2; other accounts,
    pp. 95–102; Forkel, pp. 513–14.

46 *B-Dok*, vol. 3, no. 914, p. 425; *BR*,
    p. 453; *BEST*, p. 101.

47 *Bild*, no. 149, pp.121, 371, 415;

B-Dok, vol. 2, no. 84, p. 65; *NBR*,
no. 68, p. 80; *BR*, p. 75; *BEST*, p. 103.

'VIVAT'

1 *B-Dok*, vol. 1, no. 125, pp. 200–01;
   NBR, no. 233, p. 220; *BR*, p. 172.

2 *Bild*, no. 193, pp. 141, 373, 416;
   B-Dok, vol. 2, no. 108, p. 82;
   see *NBR*, no. 86, p. 93.

3 *B-Dok*, vol. 2, no. 111, p. 83; *BEST*,
   p. 122.

4 *B-Dok*, vol. 2, no. 627, pp. 490–98;
   NBR, no. 279, pp. 250–55; *BR*,
   pp. 191–7; *BEST*, pp. 336–43.

5 *Bild*, no. 480, pp. 278, 387, 431;
   NBR, no. 310, p. 313.

6 See Wolfgang Stechow, 'Johann
   Sebastian Bach the younger', *De
   artibus opuscula*, 40: *Essays in
   honor of Erwin Panofsky*, ed.
   Millard Meiss (New York, 1961),
   pp. 427–36.

7 *B-Dok*, vol. 2, no. 423, p. 325; *NBR*,
   no. 202, p. 199; *BEST*, p. 257.

8 *B-Dok*, vol. 2, no. 458, p. 371; *NBR*,
   no. 211, p. 205; *BR*, p. 164; *BEST*,
   p. 274.

9 *B-Dok*, vol. 1, no. 50, pp. 119–20;
   NBR, no. 258, p. 235; *BR*, p. 183;
   BEST, pp. 310–11.

10 *NG*, vol. 1, p. 297. The boy was
   born on 4 October 1748, but died
   less than three weeks later.

Chapter Three
Court Composer and Teacher
(1717–1723)

1 *B-Dok*, vol. 1, no. 23, pp. 67–8;
   NBR, no. 152, p. 151; *BR*, p. 125;
   BEST, p. 191.

2 *B-Dok*, vol. 1, no. 110, p. 190; *NBR*,
   no. 70a, p. 82; *BR*, p. 76.

3 *NBR*, no. 74, p. 86; *BR*, p. 78.

4 *NBR*, no. 70b, p. 82; *BR*, p. 430.

5 *B-Dok*, vol. 1, no. 87, pp. 163–5;
   NBR, no. 72, pp. 83–5; *BR*, pp. 76–8;
   BEST, pp. 105–10.

6 *Bild*, no. 157, pp. 125, 371, 415;
   B-Dok, vol. 2, no. 94, p. 73; *NBR*,

no. 78, p. 87.

7   According to C. P. E. Bach: *B-Dok*,
    vol. 3, no. 801, p. 285; *NBR*, no. 394,
    p. 397; *BR*, p. 277; *BEST*, p. 487.
8   Forkel: *NBR*, p. 460; *BR*, p. 334;
    BEST, p. 564.
9   *B-Dok*, vol. 2, no. 100, p. 76; *NBR*,
    no. 80, p. 88; *BR*, p. 78; *BEST*, p. 111.
10 Forkel: *NBR*, p. 428; *BR*, p. 304;
    BEST, p. 515.
11 *B-Dok*, vol. 2, no. 253, pp. 186–7;
    NBR, no. 82, p. 91; *BR*, pp. 81–2;
    BEST, p. 114.
12 *Bild*, no. 193, pp. 141, 373, 416;
    B-Dok, vol. 2, no. 108, p. 82; *NBR*,
    no. 86, p. 93.
13 *Bild*, no. 194, pp. 141, 373, 416;
    B-Dok, vol. 2, no. 110, p. 83; *NBR*,
    no. 86, p. 93; *BR*, p. 83; *BEST*,
    p. 122.
14 *B-Dok*, vol. 2, no. 86, pp. 67–8;
    NBR, no. 87, p. 93; *BR*, p. 83.
15 Linnets: *B-Dok*, vol. 2. no. 477,
    p. 384; *NBR*, no. 217, p. 209; *BR*,
    pp. 166–7. Carnations: *B-Dok*,
    vol. 2, no. 423, p. 325; *NBR*,
    nos. 202, 218, pp. 199, 209; *BEST*,
    p. 257; *BR*, p. 167.
16 *B-Dok*, vol. 1, no. 23, p. 67; *NBR*,
    no. 152, p. 151 (misleading trans-
    lation); *BR*, p. 125 (misleading
    translation); *BEST*, p. 191.
17 See, for example, the recent
    Dictionnaire Mondial des Films
    (Larousse, 1999), p. 144,
    concerning Anna Magdalena: 'on
    a d'elle une chronique, peut-être
    apocryphe, qui est une sorte de
    journal intime'.
18 *NBR*, no. 94a, p. 100; *BR*, p. 88;
    BEST, p. 127.
19 *B-Dok*, vol. 2, no. 124, p. 91; *NBR*,
    no. 95, p. 101; *BEST*, p. 129.
20 *B-Dok*, vol. 2, no. 127, p. 92; *NBR*,
    no. 94c, p. 101; *BR*, p. 88; *BEST*,
    p. 130.
21 *B-Dok*, vol. 2, no. 128, p. 93; *NBR*,
    no. 96, p. 101; *BR*, p. 89; *BEST*,
    pp. 133–4.

22 Notably the separate Partitas. *Bild*,
    nos. 350–52, p. 214; *300 Jahre
    Johann Sebastian Bach, Eine
    Ausstellung der Internationalen
    Bachakademie in der Staatsgalerie
    Stuttgart* (Tutzing, Schneider, 1985),
    pp. 162–7; *NBR*, no. 127, p. 129.
23 *B-Dok*, vol. 1, no. 91, p. 174;
    no. 92, p. 17; *B-Dok*, vol. 2,
    nos. 129, 133, pp. 93, 98; *NBR*,
    nos. 97–101, pp. 102–5; *BR*,
    pp. 91–3; *BEST*, pp. 136–40.

'Drum schmauch ich…'

1   *B-Dok*, vol. 2, no. 14, p. 15; *NBR*,
    no. 19b, p. 44; *BEST*, p. 51.
2   *B-Dok*, vol. 2, no. 14, p. 15; *NBR*,
    no. 19d, p. 45; *BEST*, p. 52.
3   *BR*, pp. 97–8, both poem and
    music are unlikely to be by Bach.
4   *NBR*, no. 46b, pp. 65–6.
5   *B-Dok*, vol. 2, no. 627, pp. 490–97;
    NBR, no. 279, pp. 250–55; *BR*,
    pp. 191–7; *BEST*, pp. 336–43.

Chapter Four
Cantor and Municipal Director of
Music (1723–1750)

1   *B-Dok*, vol. 3, no. 636, p. 6; *NBR*,
    no. 311, pp. 313–14; *BR*, p. 227;
    BEST, p. 436.
2   *B-Dok*, vol. 2, no. 138, p. 104; *NBR*,
    no. 102, p. 106; *BEST*, pp. 141–2.
3   Compare *Bild*, no. 24, p. 174
    (1723) and nos. 413–14, p. 243
    (1732).
4   *B-Dok*, vol. 3, no. 803, p. 290; *NBR*,
    no. 393, p. 400; *BR*, p. 279 (trans-
    lated as 'like a beehive'); *BEST*,
    p. 490.
5   The photographs are now in the
    Bach-Archiv, Leipzig. *Bild*, nos.
    418, 420, pp. 245–7, 384, 428. See
    also Ulrich Leisinger, *Bach in
    Leipzig* (Leipzig, Edition Leipzig,
    1998), pp. 24–33.
6   *Bild*, no. 266, pp. 176, 376, 420.
7   Photograph in Leisinger, *op. cit.*,
    p. 24.

8 *B-Dok*, vol. 2, no. 139, p. 104; *NBR*, no. 103, p. 106; *BR*, p. 93; *BEST*, pp. 142–3.

9 *B-Dok*, vol. 2, no. 144, p. 106; *NBR*, no. 104, pp. 106–8; *BR*, pp. 93–5; *BEST*, pp. 143–4.

10 *Bild*, no. 250a, pp. 168, 375, 419.

11 *Bild*, no. 250b, pp. 168, 375, 419.

12 *Bild*, no. 134, pp. 112, 370, 414.

13 Charles Mould, 'The tabel harpsichord', *Keyboard Instruments: Studies in Keyboard Organology, 1500–1800*, ed. Edwin M. Ripin (Edinburgh, Edinburgh University Press, 1971; reprint New York, Dover, 1977), p. 64, plates 50, 52.

14 *B-Dok*, vol. 2, no. 149, p. 112; *NBR*, no. 111, p. 112; *BEST*, p. 145.

15 1754 obituary: *B-Dok*, vol. 3, no. 666, p. 86; *NBR*, no. 306, p. 304; *BR*, p. 221; *BEST*, p. 475.

16 See Alfred Dürr, 'Zur Chronologie der Leipziger Vokalwerke J. S. Bachs', *Bach Jahrbuch*, 44 (1957). Revised version republished separately (Kassel, 1976).

17 *B-Dok*, vol. 2, no. 179, p. 139; *NBR*, no. 115, p. 116; *BR*, pp. 96–7; *BEST*, pp. 153–4.

18 *B-Dok*, vol. 1, no. 179, p. 249; *NBR*, no. 115, p. 116; *BEST*, p. 155.

19 *B-Dok*, vol. 1, note to no. 179, pp. 249–50; *B-Dok*, vol. 2, no. 182, p. 142; *BEST*, p. 155.

20 There remains a slight doubt about this date of first performance. Bach certainly performed the work on Good Friday (15 April) 1729. See *NBR*, no. 114, p. 115.

21 Several other German composers later adopted the same title, partly in homage to Bach: Georg Andreas Sorge (3 volumes, 1738–45, the third of which is dedicated to Bach), Friedrich Gottlob Fleischer (1745), Georg Joachim Hahn (*c*.1746), Karl Christoph Hachmeister (*c*.1750), Johann

Ludwig Krebs (3 volumes, *c*.1750–60), Marianus Königsperger (1760) and Johann Philipp Kirnberger (1761).

22 *B-Dok*, vol. 1, no. 23, pp. 67–8; *NBR*, no. 152, p. 152; *BR*, pp. 125–6; *BEST*, pp. 190–92.

23 *B-Dok*, vol. 2, no. 232, p. 175; *NBR*, no. 136, p. 136; *BR*, p. 113; *BEST*, p. 171.

24 *B-Dok*, vol. 1, no. 19, pp. 54–5; *NBR*, no. 138, p. 137–8; *BR*, pp. 114–15; *BEST*, pp. 175–6.

25 *B-Dok*, vol. 2, no. 280, p. 205; *NBR*, no. 150, p. 145; *BR*, pp. 119–20; *BEST*, pp. 183–4.

26 *B-Dok*, vol. 1, no. 22, pp. 60–66; *NBR*, no. 151, pp. 145–51; *BR*, pp. 120–24; *BEST*, pp. 184–90.

27 *B-Dok*, vol. 1, no. 23, pp. 67–8; *NBR*, no. 152, pp. 151–2; *BR*, pp. 125–6; *BEST*, pp. 190–92.

28 *B-Dok*, vol. 1, no. 69, p. 138; *NBR*, no. 154, p. 153; *BR*, pp. 126–7.

29 *B-Dok*, vol. 1, no. 27, p. 74; *NBR*, no. 162, p. 158; *BR*, pp. 128–9; *BEST*, p. 203.

30 J. S. Riemer: *B-Dok*, vol. 2, no. 352, p. 250; *NBR*, no. 173, p. 166; *BR*, p. 433; *BEST*, pp. 208–9.

31 *B-Dok*, vol. 1, no. 184, pp. 255–67; *NBR*, no. 303, pp. 283–94; *BR*, pp. 203–11; *BEST*, pp. 25–40. These versions are based on the copy by C. P. E. Bach's daughter, Anna Carolina Philippina. Another (older?) version has recently come to light in the Bach archives rediscovered in 1999 in the Ukraine.

32 *B-Dok*, vol. 1, no. 38, pp. 93–4; *NBR*, no. 189, p. 187; *BR*, pp. 150–51; *BEST*, p. 236.

33 *B-Dok*, vol. 1, no. 63, p. 131; *NBR*, no. 142, p. 141; *BR*, p. 117.

34 This phrase, it should be noted, is reported only by Ernesti in his reply of 17 August. *B-Dok*, vol. 2, no. 382, p. 272; *NBR*, no. 184, p. 180; *BR*, p. 144; *BEST*, p. 228.

35 *B-Dok*, vol. 1, nos 32–4, pp. 82–8; *NBR*, nos. 181–3, pp. 172–6; *BR*, pp. 137–41; *BEST*, pp. 219–24.

36 *B-Dok*, vol. 1, no. 34, p. 87; *NBR*, no. 183, p. 175; *BR*, p. 140; *BEST*, p. 223.

37 *B-Dok*, vol. 2, nos. 382, 383, pp. 268–76; *NBR*, no. 186, p. 185; *BR*, pp. 141–9; *BEST*, pp. 224–33.

38 *B-Dok*, vol. 1, no. 40, pp. 99–100; *NBR*, no. 192, pp. 189–90; *BR*, p. 152.

39 *B-Dok*, vol. 1, no. 39, pp. 95–6; *NBR*, no. 193, p. 190; *BR*, pp. 153–4.

40 *B-Dok*, vol. 1, no. 40, pp. 97–8; *NBR*, no. 194, p. 192; *BR*, pp. 154–6.

41 *B-Dok*, vol. 1, no. 41, pp. 101–2; *NBR*, no. 195, p. 194; *BR*, pp. 156–7; *BEST*, p. 244.

42 *B-Dok*, vol. 2, no. 592, p. 462; *NBR*, no. 28, p. 241; *BEST*, p. 325.

43 *B-Dok*, vol. 2, no. 400, p. 286; *NBR*, no. 343, p. 338; *BR*, p. 238; *BEST*, pp. 241–2.

44 *B-Dok*, vol. 2, no. 409, p. 296; *NBR*, no. 344, p. 338–48; *BR*, pp. 239–47; *BEST*, p. 248–50.

45 *B-Dok*, vol. 2, no. 413, p. 309; *NBR*, no. 345, p. 348; *BR*, pp. 247–8; *BEST*, pp. 252–3.

46 *B-Dok*, vol. 2, no. 420, p. 322; *NBR*, no. 345, p. 348; *BR*, pp. 248–9.

47 *B-Dok*, vol. 2, no. 442, pp. 360–62; *NBR*, no. 347, pp. 350–52; *BR*, pp. 249–51.

48 *B-Dok*, vol. 2, no. 533, pp. 417–19; *NBR*, no. 348, p. 353; *BR*, p. 212.

49 The whole episode was still remembered over 30 years later. J. F. Agricola, who had studied with Bach between 1738 and 1741, refers to it in a letter dated 11 November 1771: *B-Dok*, vol. 3, no. 762, p. 211; *BEST*, p. 444. And Forkel also mentions it: *NBR*, p. 440; *BR*, p. 316; *BEST*, p. 534.

50 *B-Dok*, vol. 1, nos. 42–3, pp. 107–10; *NBR*, nos. 203–4,

pp. 200–02; *BR*, pp. 160–61; *BEST*, pp. 260–61.

51 *B-Dok*, vol. 2, no. 439, pp. 338–9; *NBR*, no. 208, p. 204; *BR*, pp. 162–3; *BEST*, p. 265.

52 Bach's illness (November 1739): *B-Dok*, vol. 2, no. 462, p. 373; *NBR*, no. 212, pp. 205–6; *BEST*, pp. 274–5. Anna Magdalena's illness (August/September 1741), involving 'the most acute pains of the body': *B-Dok*, vol. 2, nos. 489–90, pp. 391–2; *NBR*, nos. 222–3, pp. 212–13; *BR*, pp. 168–9; *BEST*, pp. 281–2.

53 *B-Dok*, vol. 2, no. 554, p. 434; *NBR*, no. 239, p. 224; *BR*, p. 176; *BEST*, pp. 298–9.

54 1754 obituary: *B-Dok*, vol. 3, no. 666, p. 85; *NBR*, no. 306, pp. 302–3; *BR*, p. 220; *BEST*, pp. 473–4.

55 Forkel: *NBR*, p. 429; *BR*, pp. 305–6; *BEST*, pp. 516–17.

56 Helped in part by his younger brother Johann Heinrich; see Wolfgang Wiemer, *Die wiederhergestellte Ordnung in Johann Sebastian Bachs Kunst der Fuge* (Wiesbaden, Breitkopf & Härtel, 1977), pp. 40–45, and Christoph Wolff, ed., *Das musicalisches Opfer*, facsimile edition (Leipzig, Peters, 1977), 'Addendum'.

57 Letter to Johann Elias Bach, 6 October 1748: *B-Dok*, vol. 1, no. 49, pp. 117–18; *NBR*, no. 257, p. 234; *BR*, p. 182; *BEST*, p. 309. See also below note 61.

58 Wolff, *Das musicalisches Opfer*, p. 13.

59 *Bild*, no. 565, p. 319. The full list of other members of this learned corresponding society were, in order of joining: founding members in 1739: (1) Count Giacomo de Lucchesini, (2) Lorenz Mizler himself, (3) Georg Heinrich Bümler of Brandenburg,

(4) Christoph Gottlieb Schröter of Nordhausen, (5) Heinrich Bockemeyer of Wolfenbüttel, (6) Georg Philipp Telemann of Hamburg, (7) Gottfried Heinrich Stölzel of Gotha; 1742: (8) Georg Friedrich Lingke of Bergrath, 1743: (9) Fr Meinradus Spiess, an abbot, (10) Georg Vensky of Brandenburg, 1745: (11) Georg Friedrich Haendel of London, (12) Fr Udalricus Weiss, a Benedictine monk, 1746: (13) Carl Heinrich Graun of Berlin, 1747: (14) Johann Sebastian Bach, (15) Georg Andreas Sorge, (16) Johann Paul Kuntzen, 1748: (17) Christian Friedrich Fischer, 1751: (18) Johann Christian Winter, 1752: (19) Johann Georg Kaltenbeck.

60 See the paragraph added by Mizler at the end of the 1754 obituary: *B-Dok*, vol. 3, no. 666, pp. 88–9; *NBR*, no. 306, p. 307; *BR*, p. 224; *BEST*, pp. 478–9.

61 Evidence suggests that his second official offering may have been very much more modest than the first, being the 'six in three' canon, BWV 1087/13, that appears in the 1746 Haussmann portrait. Two copies of the separate published version survive (*Bild*, no. 563, pp. 318, 391, 434–5); see also the paragraph added by Mizler at the end of the 1754 obituary: *B-Dok*, vol. 3, no. 666, pp. 88–9; *NBR*, no. 306, p. 307; *BR*, p. 224; *BEST*, pp. 478–9. However Bach could also have given away copies of the ricercars to members of the society (at that date this would have required sixteen other copies since Sorge, Kuntzen and Fischer had also since joined; see note 59).

62 *B-Dok*, vol. 3, no. 659, p. 73; *NBR*, no. 354a, p. 361; *BR*, p. 255; *BEST*, p. 439.

63 *B-Dok*, vol. 3, no. 701, pp. 144–5; *NBR*, no. 357a, p. 363; *BR*, p. 257; *BEST*, p. 387.

64 *NBR*, p. 465; *BR*, p. 339; *BEST*, p. 572.

65 *Bild*, 'B1', p. 11. At present on display in the old Town Hall in Leipzig.

66 *Bild*, 'B2', p. 12. At present belonging to William H. Scheide, Princeton, New Jersey.

67 Wiemer, *Die wiederhergestellte Ordnung*, pp. 39–49.

68 See Gregory Butler, 'Ordering problems in J. S. Bach's "Art of Fugue" resolved', *Musical Quarterly* (Winter 1983).

'Quaerendo invenietis'

1 *Bild*, no. 142, pp. 116, 371, 414; *NBR*, no. 45, p. 66; *BR*, pp. 64, 400, 429.

2 *Bild*, no. 432, pp. 253, 385, 428; *NBR*, no. 133, p. 135; *BR*, pp. 111, 402. In 1732, Hudemann published a poem in honour of Bach: *B-Dok*, vol. 2, no. 325; *BR*, p. 226; *BEST*, pp. 198–9.

3 *Bild*, no. 439, pp. 256, 385, 429; *NBR*, no. 166, p. 162; *BR*, pp. 131, 402–3.

4 *Bild*, no. 585, pp. 330, 392, 436; *NBR*, no. 259, pp. 236–7; *BR*, pp. 184, 406–7.

Chapter Five
28 July 1750

1 *B-Dok*, vol. 2, no. 598, p. 468; *NBR*, no. 269, p. 243; *BR*, p. 437; *BEST*, p. 319.

2 *B-Dok*, vol. 3, no. 712, p. 171; *NBR*, no. 270, p. 244; *BR*, pp. 187–8; *BEST*, p. 320. The reference to

cataracts occurs in an article published in May 1750: *B-Dok*, vol. 2, no. 601, p. 470; *BEST*, p. 322.

3 *B-Dok*, vol. 2, no. 601, p. 470; *BEST*, p. 322.

4 1754 obituary: *B-Dok*, vol. 3, no. 666, p. 85; *NBR*, no. 306, p. 303; *BR*, p. 220; *BEST*, p. 474.

5 *B-Dok*, vol. 3, no. 848, p. 340; *NBR*, no. 405, p. 412; *BR*, p. 291; *BEST*, p. 364.

6 *B-Dok*, vol. 2, no. 583, p. 456; *NBR*, no. 265, p. 240; *BR*, p. 185; *BEST*, p. 316.

7 1754 obituary: *B-Dok*, vol. 3, no. 666, p. 85; *NBR*, no. 306, p. 303; *BR*, p. 220; *BEST*, p. 474.

8 *B-Dok*, vol. 2, no. 323, p. 231; *NBR*, no. 304, p. 294; *BR*, p. 46; *BEST*, p. 197. The original statement is recorded in Walther's *Lexicon*, p. 64. A list of over 400 compositions based on this famous theme, compiled by Ulrich Prinz, Joachim Dorfmüller and Konrad Küster, may be found in *300 Jahre Johann Sebastian Bach*. This includes some works that predate *The Art of Fugue*, such as the *Fuga sub Diatessaron La Guide è pra soil Nome del celebre Signor Bach* by Bach's friend, the Dresden organist Christian Petzold.

9 *Bild*, no. 616, pp. 342, 394, 438; *NBR*, no. 298, p. 275 (also no. 285, p. 260).

10 Preface by Marpurg to second edition, 1752: *B-Dok*, vol. 3, no. 648, p. 15; *NBR*, no. 374, p. 376; *BR*, p. 267; *BEST*, p. 416. The 'friend' was Altnikol, according to Forkel: *NBR*, p. 466; *BR*, p. 340; *BEST*, p. 573.

11 1754 obituary: *B-Dok*, vol. 3, no. 666, p. 85; *NBR*, no. 306, p. 303; *BR*, p. 220; *BEST*, p. 474.

12 *B-Dok*, vol. 2, no. 605, p. 472; *BEST*, p. 325.

13 Confusion has arisen about the exact time. In the 1754 obituary, C. P. E. Bach says 'des Abends nach einem Viertel auf 9 Uhr' (*B-Dok*, vol. 3, p. 85). The *BR* (p. 220) wrongly translates this as 8.45 p.m.: 'a little after a quarter to nine in the evening'. *BEST* (p. 474) gives a different mistranslation, 9.15 p.m.: 'à neuf heures un quart du soir'. However in old German usage (confirmed in dictionaries of the period) 'nach einem Viertel auf 9 Uhr' means at 8.15 p.m., a time which is in accordance with Abraham Kriegel's comment on the day itself, that Bach died 'at 8 o'clock' (see note 11). *NBR* (no. 306, p. 303) gives the correct time.

14 *B-Dok*, vol. 2, no. 607, p. 473; *BEST*, pp. 325–6.

15 *B-Dok*, vol. 2, no. 615, p. 480; *NBR*, no. 274b, p. 247; *BR*, p. 439.

16 *B-Dok*, vol. 2, no. 615, p. 480; *NBR*, no. 274b, pp. 246–7; *BR*, p. 438; *BEST*, p. 330.

17 *B-Dok*, vol. 2, no. 615, p. 480; *NBR*, no. 274b, p. 247; *BR*, p. 439; *BEST*, p. 330.

18 *B-Dok*, vol. 2, no. 611, p. 475; *NBR*, no. 272, pp. 244–5; *BR*, p. 188; *BEST*, p. 327.

19 *B-Dok*, vol. 2, no. 609, p. 474; *NBR*, no. 271, p. 244; *BR*, p. 188; *BEST*, p. 328.

20 The 'Specificatio': *B-Dok*, vol. 2, no. 627, pp. 490–97; *NBR*, no. 279, pp. 250–55; *BR*, pp. 191–7; *BEST*, pp. 336–43.

21 Albert Schweitzer, *J. S. Bach*, English translation by Ernest Newman from the 1908 German edition, vol. 1 (London, Breitkopf and Härtel, 1911; reprint, London, A. & C. Black, 1962), p. 162.

22 *Bild*, no. 620, pp. 345, 394, 438.

23 *B-Dok*, vol. 3, no. 1032, p. 594; *BEST*, p. 464.

24 *NBR*, p. 33; *BR*, p. 371.

25 Schweitzer, *Bach*, vol. 1, pp. 162–3.

The report by Wilhelm His to the
Leipzig town council was entitled
Johann Sebastian Bach:
Forschungen über dessen
Grabstätte, Gebeine und Antlitz
(Leipzig, F. C. W. Vogel). See also
the report published in
Musikalische Wochenblatt
(Jahrgang 26, 1895), pp. 339–40
and *Allgemeine Musikzeitung*
(1895), pp. 384ff.

Index